CINNAMON

CINNAMON

Cynthia A. Thomas

PALMETTO
PUBLISHING
Charleston, SC
www.PalmettoPublishing.com

Hardcover ISBN: 979-8-8229-4772-6
Paperback ISBN: 979-8-8229-4773-3

CONTENTS

DEDICATION

"To you, dear reader, for making this journey worthwhile." "For my readers, who suffer from addiction, and Mental Illness due to childhood trauma. To the one who breathe life into these pages " "To all those who pick up this book, thank you for giving my words a chance." "For every reader to find piece within themselves throughout these chapters."

RIP
Terrance "DOX" Thomas
06/27/82 - 03/20/19
Veronica D. Thomas (MOMMY)
03/27/63 - 01/27/21
James "Sameo Jameo" Santiago
05/20/77 - 01/12/20

PROLOGUE

It was a gloomy, cloudy Sunday afternoon when Cinnamon frantically stormed out of her trailer with blood gushing from the top of her head, a black eye, and a swollen lip. Her jumbo box braids were drenched with blood, and identifying her would have been impossible due to the boundless size of her swollen upper and lower lips. She wore an all-black sundress with black flip-flops. She stood at five feet three inches, and she weighed 185 pounds, thick in all the right places.

Guys loved the way she looked because not only was she gorgeous, but her eyes were hypnotizing. She and her husband got into a heated argument which led to him viciously beating her ass for hours. This was nothing new, they occasionally fought like cats and dogs after a night out of drinking, partying, snorting,popping pills, and smoking marijuana. Her husband demanded her to be ready to get fucked when he come back from taking a piss. Something hit her like a wave once she heard the bathroom door slam shut. Something told her to get her up, and get the hell out of there.

Running out of their house like a madwoman, Cinnamon anxiously jumped into their black navigator truck that was parked in the yard.

Feeling terrified of the thought of her husband and what he would do once he realized she wasn't in the house caused her entire body to tremble with fear. Quickly cranking up the truck, and before she could drive up the devil emerged.

Enraged, her husband came running out of the house like a mad man. *Oh hell, he's going to fucking kill me,* Cinnamon thought as she turned the keys in the ignition, and sped off.

"Yeah, bitch, go be with that nigga; do what you do best and go suck some dick," he angrily yelled at the top of his lungs. See, Raheem was the type who always had to be right and could do no wrong. He was territorial, viciously jealous, and physically, sexually, emotionally abusive.

He stood at 5-feet 11-inches with a 145-pound frame, and had long hair that he kept braided for as long as Cinnamon had known him. They had been together for seven years and married for only four months.

Their relationship has been rocky since day one, and getting married was the worst decision she's ever made. Everybody seemed to know this except Cinnamon.

She drove around Claiborne County until the gas hand landed on "E". Before she knew it, she started to have an anxiety attack. A few years back, she was diagnosed with anxiety and depression. Drugs, sex and alcohol was her antidote; all her problems seem to come down on her all at once. She has been in denial and blind to all the things that were going on in her life. She was oblivious to the fact that she was the cause of all her troubles.

For the past few years she abused drugs and alcohol to suppress her pain. Little did she know that on that particular Sunday morning it would be the starting point of the chaos that was to come.

She could feel this demonic presence that tormented her throughout her entire life hovering over her body. She approached a dead end road and she placed the truck in park. She reached over to the passenger seat, went into her purse, and slowly pulled out her gun.

You'll never be anything; just do it; go ahead and take yourself out. Nobody loves you, not even your own mother and father.

These are the thoughts that ran through her mind as she sat in her truck with her 45 pistol pressed against the left side of her head. She was devastated because life at age twenty-eight was not how she expected it to be. She felt as though she was in hell, and the best description of what she was experiencing would be the feeling of being worthless, lost and hopeless.

Her best friend was out of her life, her marriage was a disaster, her family could care less about her, she lost custody of her 2 boys, and to top it off, she was battling addiction along with mental disorders. She sat in the driver's seat with tears flowing down her face. "I can't do this shit anymore. I want out," she said to herself with slob and snot pouring from her nose and mouth.

She held the gun to her head while sobbing, "Babies, Mommy will always love you, and I'm so sorry. Please forgive me." She then closed her eyes and pulled the trigger. "CLICK" was the sound that she heard as she realized that she wasn't dead.

She was so belligerent that she didn't realize that the clip of the gun was next to her in the passenger seat. "WTF!!" she yelled as she angrily punched her fist into the steering wheel. She reached over to the passenger seat and snatched the clip and placed it into the gun and cocked it back.

She closed her eyes, placed the gun on the right side of her neck and proceeded to slowly start a countdown starting from 3 ... 2, and before she could say 1, she heard a voice in her head that told her she was forgiven for all her sins, and she had a chance to make everything right.

That voice also told her that she had a second chance to get her life together, to be strong and live righteous, and that good things will follow.

That voice gave her the feeling of calmness, and within that calmness a big weight was lifted off of her shoulders. She sat there thinking about her life, about the people she hurt, and took advantage of. That's when she became curious to know how, and where the root of this curse began. Then suddenly, out of nowhere she passed out from exhaustion, and drifted off into a place that she called "The Dark Ages." The reason being because this is when darkness gave its barbaric introduction. It began in the winter of 1988, when Cinnamon was only a year and a half years old.

CHAPTER 1

THE DARK AGES

M s. Stalks turnt the shower off after hearing the phone ring consecutively for five minutes. "It better be important" she told herself as she hastily stepped out of the shower, grabbed her purple robe and quickly ran into the living room to answer the phone.

"Hello!" said Mona while trying to catch her breath. "Yes, Umm may I speak to Ms. Mona Stalks please?" said the lady on the other end of the phone with a strong Spanish accent. "Yes, this is her,"Mona politely said "how can I help you?".

"Well, hello. My name is Dr. Hernandez, and I'm calling from Harlem Hospital. "I really need to speak to you in person as soon as possible," said Dr. Hernandez.

"Her English is horrible," Mona thought to herself as she curiously wondered why this lady was calling her, and to top it off, wanted her to come all the way to Harlem Hospital. It had to have been something serious, and Mona was anxious to figure out what it was.

"May I ask what this is concerning?" she asked while trying her hardest not to sound rude.

Dr. Hernandez paused for a second trying to figure out how she was going to tell Mona that she had to come get custody of her newborn granddaughter who tested positive for drugs and alcohol. Dr. Hernandez quickly decided that it would be best to discuss this matter in person.

"I'm unauthorized to discuss this matter over the phone but I will say that it's concerning your granddaughter, as well as your daughter Virginia Stalks". Mona was speechless as Dr. Hernandez continued to say what she had to say. "I will be here until seven p.m, my office is located on the 10th floor ok? well goodbye" Dr. Hernandez politely said before hanging up the phone.

What the hell did this girl get herself into now? was the question that kept running through Mona's head. It literally took her less than fifteen minutes to get dressed and hop on the bus.

The twenty-minute bus ride to the hospital felt like an eternity to Mona.

When she arrived she anxiously walked up to the front desk to get some information from the receptionist. "Hi, I'm Ms. Stalks, and I'm here to see Dr. Hernandez." The receptionist was teary eyed and had to have been on the phone with an ex-boyfriend or someone because she was filled with emotion. "Well, I need to see my kids; you can't do this to me! You know they need their mother as much as they need their father" the receptionist furiously said as she completely ignored Mona.

"Hello? Hello?!!!" Mona aggressively shouted, banging her hand on the receptionist desk. The receptionist was a Puerto Rican girl who was petite and very pretty. She barely noticed that Mona was in front of her desk due to the heated discussion she was having.

"Oh, I apologize, It's my crazy ex-husband he's driving me crazy," the receptionist said as she hung up the phone as fast as she could.

She looked at Mona and said, "Well, Dr. Hernandez's office is Located on the 10th floor, walk straight ahead the elevator will be on the right."

"Thank you," said Mona as she quickly walked down the hallway and into the elevator.

She approached the 10th floor and noticed Dr.Hernandez office on the left side of the hallway. The door was slightly ajar, so she knocked on the door and slowly walked in. "Hi, I'm Mona Stalks, and we talked on the phone less than a hour ago."

"Yes, I remember," Dr. Hernandez said as she stood up and pointed to the chair in front of her desk directing Mona to have a seat . The best way to describe Dr. Hernandez would be drop dead gorgeous. Better yet drop dead gorgeous will be an understatement. Dr. Hernandez was stunning. She stood about 5'9 with a petite body frame. She had hazel eyes, beautiful skin, long black shiny hair, she was a Cuban goddess.

With her strong Cuban accent, Dr. Hernandez proceeded to say,"Yes, have a seat ma'am, and let me tell you the reason why I ask you here today," with a serious look on her face she stated "I'm here to inform you that your daughter Virginia Stalks gave birth to a baby on the twentieth of this month." Stated Dr. Hernández as she looked through her papers to make sure that the information she was given Mona was accurate.

She looked Mona in her eyes and said, "we informed your daughter Virginia that she was unauthorized to leave the hospital with her baby.

The reason for that was because we found narcotics in the child's system". Words cannot describe the expression on Mona's face as she sat there listening to what was being told to her. "I've noticed that she had put your name and number down as a person to contact in case of emergency" Dr. Hernandez stated. "It has been very difficult to get in contact with families of the child, so the decision was made to place the baby in the care of child protective services tomorrow if we were not successful in contacting immediate family members.

Mona was speechless which was not in her character because she always had something to say. "I hope it wasn't an inconvenience asking you to come here," said Doctor Hernandez who was semi-curious as to why Mona has not yet responded to anything she was saying.

Mona was astounded throughout the entire meeting, she felt like she was dreaming.

"We understand that Virginia has two other children?," Dr. Hernandez stated prior to grabbing the yellow folder from the upper left side of her desk. She opened the folder and proceeded to pull out some documents.

"Okay, well yes, I see here that she has a one year old named Cinnamon Stalks, and a five-year-old son named Travon Stalks. "Unfortunately, they also have to be removed from Virginia's custody" Dr. Hernandez told her while she continued to ramble through the paperwork. They sat there in silence as It took a few minutes for Mona to process all of the information that was just given to her. "Can you excuse me for a second?" Dr. Hernandez asked while she stood up and walked out of her office.

A load of guilt hit Mona, all at once she began to feel guilty because she knew she wasn't the best parent in the world. She knew that she was the root of her dysfunctional family. Everyone has a story, and Mona's story is that she had four sons and four daughters; half of her kids were either child molesters, drug addicts, or licentious.

It started in 1970 when Mona relocated from her home town Mississippi to Brooklyn, New York. She fell head over heels in love with a hoodlum named Bernard Jones. Bernard was originally born and raised in Atlanta Georgia. Tired of the physical, and sexual abuse from his father, Benard ran away from home at the age of thirteen. He slept anywhere he could lay his head and made money by doing sexual favors with old men. To escape the memory of his childhood he decided to hitch a ride to Brooklyn, New York. He may have left the country, but the country never left his ass. Benard believed that a woman should know her place and stay in it. He felt that a woman's place was beneath a man, and if a woman disobeyed her man, she should get viciously beaten.

Silly fucking rabbit I don't know who the hell he thought he was.

Anyways, Mona met Bernard one hot summer afternoon when she and a co-worker visited the Bronx zoo. Mona and her friend were giggling and laughing at the monkeys when someone crept up behind her and whispered in her ear" Is your bathwater as sweet as you are? I would love to get a taste". Mona turned around and it was Benard standing there dressed in a sky blue tailor made suit and sky blue alligator shoes. After conversing for a while they exchanged numbers and have been inseparable ever since. It didn't take long for them to have a connection. It was something about Benard that made Mona love him more and more each day.

After a few months into their relationship, she had to learn the hard way that Benard was sexually, mentally, and physically abusive. One night, they decided to go out to a bar. Mona's favorite song came on "*Sexual healing*" by Marvin Gaye. Mona, being herself, got up and ran to the dance floor. She wanted to impress Benard so she slowly rocked her hips from side to side while seductively licking her lips.

She turned around to see if her boo Bernard was checking her out, and noticed the chair he was sitting in was empty. She continued to dance until the song was finished. Mona searched around looking for Benard, but he was nowhere in sight. She grabbed her jacket and headed towards the exit to see if he was outside. Mona walked over to his car and noticed Benard was in his Cadillac, smoking a cigarette. She slowly opened the door and got into the car. Before she could close the door, she got a fist to the face, not only that she also got her head smashed in the dashboard. He cursed her out calling her all types of whores and sluts as he drove the both of them home.

Mona cried the whole ride home as Bernard curse her out like she was a dog in the streets .Once they were inside their apartment Benard stood by the front door for a few seconds with this demonic look on his face.

That's when hell broke loose, and Benard grabbed Mona by her hair and dragged her down the hallway towards the bedroom.

Once they entered the bedroom Benard viciously slapped her across the face before throwing her on the bed. He then aggressively ripped off her dress ignoring the sounds of Mona begging and pleading for him to stop. Little did she know that the sounds of her crying, and pleading for him to stop sexually turn him on. Bernard sexually, and physically assaulted Mona for hours. He told her that fucking her in the asa was her punishment for dancing like a slut. He mad it clear that he was not the one to fuck with.

After he was done, he grabbed her by the hair and calmly said, "go wash your nasty ass, then bring that ass back to bed."

Disgusted and afraid Mona shamefully did exactly what she was told. That was the first time Benard assaulted her , and sadly that will not be the last.

Mona endured Bernard's abuse for seventeen years, and to make matters worse, she had six children with him.. Not only was she being physically and sexually abused her children endured the abuse as well.

Mona was extremely concerned about her children's safety when she witnessed Benard molesting their 4 year old daughter. Well let's just say that she witnessed bruises on her daughter's inner thighs, as well as blood stains in her panties.Weeks later, Mona's son opened up to Mona discussing how Benard touched him in his private area.

Too fearful to remove her and her children from that toxic environment, she came up with a plan to remove the children only.

Mona knew for a fact that Bernard would find her and kill her if she ever left him. Mona miraculously convinced Benard that they would be able to party more and spend more time together if the kids were to go to Mississippi to stay with her parents, he agreed.

The sexual and physical abuse Mona and Bernard's children endured affected them for the rest of their lives. By the time Mona realized this, the damage had been fully done.

Dr. Hernandez walked back into her office carrying stacks of brown folders. "I apologize for the interruption" Dr. Hernandez stated while placing the stacks of folders on the top of her desk. She glanced over at Mona to see if she was going to respond. *"Ms. Stalks......Mona Stalks......... Ms. Sta̶lks!"*

Dr.Hernandez yelled before sitting down at her desk. Mona was startled by Dr. Hernandez and slightly embarrassed about her behavior.

That Trip down memory lane gave Mona the chills, so she shook it off, and cleared her throat. *"Please forgive me. I'm very sorry, I was mentally processing everything"*,said Mona.

"Oh it's okay, no need to apologize", said Dr. Hernandez.

Mona looked directly into Dr. Hernandez eyes and said, "Whatever it is that you need me to do, let me know and it will be done."

"Okay, great!" Dr.Hernandez stated in her strong Spanish accent.

"Well let's get it started, here are some documents I need you to sign" She told Mona as she placed the four sheets of papers along with a pen in front of Mona.

After the paperwork was completed Hernandez looked at Mona and asked her if she would like to see her beautiful granddaughter?" "Yes, umm yeah," Mona nervously replied in a calm but anxious voice. "Well, follow me right this way," said Ms. Hernandez.

She led Mona out of her office and around the corner to the nursery. "There she is, the last baby on the right," said Dr.. Hernandez as she pressed her finger against the glass. "The one that's doing all that fussing and crying ?" Mona asked.

Dr. Hernandez looked Mona in her eyes and said, "I'm sorry to inform you but it's going to be a challenge for a while. Your granddaughter is going through withdrawal which means that she will have some side effects from the crack cocaine that's in her system. Her crying will be ten times worse than a normal baby; she will have the shakes and tremors for a few weeks..

It didn't matter to Mona, as she instantly fell in love with her beautiful chocolate-chip granddaughter. She weighed only three pounds—so small that you could hold her in the palm of your hands. After visiting the baby Dr.Hernandez led Mona to the elevator. They said goodbye to each other, and within three weeks, she had full custody of all three grandkids. The newborn baby was named Little Virginia , Cinnamon who was a year and a half and Tavon who was five-years-old.

Mona didn't think twice about gaining custody of her grandchildren. She kind of felt as if God was giving her another chance to be a better mother than she was with her own children. It didn't take long for her to stop hanging out at the liquor store or the L-I-Q store as Mona would call it. LOL.

Mona changed a lot of her old ways for the sake and lives of her grandchildren. What didn't change within her was her guilt towards the way she allowed her children to be mistreated by their father.

Speaking of Benard who has received bad karma in a way that he very much so deserved.When Mona would attempt to leave Bernard, he would tell her that death was the only way out. Unfortunately he was right, death came in the worst way possible. It skipped Mona and landed on this young lady Bernard started to date after him and Mona's breakup. Bernard choked the breath out of the young lady before throwing her out of his 14th floor window. Bernard was sentenced to life in prison without the chance of Parole.

Since Mona was going to be raising her three grandchildren, she decided to leave her one bedroom apartment and move into a bigger apartment.

Mona was relieved, but at the same time she felt sympathy for the young lady and her family. Mona was finally free and blessed to have Bernard permanently out of her life.

Since Mona was going to be raising her three grandchildren, she decided to leave her one bedroom apartment and move into a bigger apartment. She received a 3 bedroom apartment in Castle Hill Projects.

Between working and providing for three kids Mona didn't know how she was going to be able to do all of these things by herself. She came up with the idea to let her kids come back to New York so they can help her with her three grandchildren.

When her kids graduated high school, they left Mississippi and relocated to New York. Mona's children were excited about rebuilding their relationship with Mona without Bernard's evil presence.

Mona worked the graveyard shift, so Lil Virginia, Cinnamon and Tavon were left with their uncles and aunts.Mona was a home health aide, and she would leave for work around 8:00 p.m. and wouldn't get home until 8:00 a.m.

All types of chaos would occur the moment she walked out of her apartment.

Mona's kids were aged from eighteen to twenty-four years old, and they loved partying, sex, and drugs.

One thing they didn't like was having to watch little Virginia, Cinnamon, and Tavon. It was like they couldn't fathom why Mona was raising her grandchildren when she didn't raise them.They felt like the kids were not their responsibility and Virginia needed to come raise her own children. This feeling of envy, hate and jealousy began to emerge. Deep down inside they were envious of the fact that Mona decided to raise her grandchildren. They urged Virginia to get herself together so she could be a good mother to her children instead of choosing drugs over everything important. If that's not bad enough, how about Virginia being a no show for the custody hearing.

With that being said, the kids were left without a mother as well as a father.Their father came around and visited once so often until an incident occurred that stopped him from coming around.

It was Christmas, and he had bought each of the kids' name chains that were very popular at the time. The chains were stolen and pawned by their dope fiend uncles, and the other was broken into pieces by one of the aunts named Bernice who was very evil and physically abusive towards the kids. When the kids father heard about it he confronted Bernice. That confrontation resulted in him being hospitalized with two broken ribs and a fractured jaw. It took years before the kids saw their father again.

Bernice thought she was better than the rest of the family because she was the only child that didn't receive any kind of sexual or physical abuse from her father Bernard. She was the only child that he truly loved.

She was very short; she stood at five feet, two inches, cute face, and petite body, with one of the nastiest attitudes known to mankind. For some reason, she hated Cinnamon with a passion so much that she nicknamed Cinnamon's "Red Hefa." Bernice also hated that she had to share her bed with Cinnamon, if it was left up to her Cinnamon would have been sleeping on the floor. One Saturday morning, Bernice woke up and found her bed soaking wet with urine. "I know this Red Hefa did not piss in my damn bed. "Where the hell are you?" Bernice yelled as loud as she could.

"Red Hefa!!" she yelled as she viciously searched every room in the apartment. "When I find you I'm a kill your nasty ass!!" Bernice said as she angrily stormed into the kitchen.

Cinnamon was frantically hiding under the kitchen table, scared out of her mind because she knew exactly what Bernice was going to do when she found her.

Cinnamon started to tremble as she could hear Bernice footsteps getting closer and closer.

"There you go," Bernice said as she reached down and grabbed Cinnamon by her hair and pulled her up from underneath the table. Five-year-old Cinnamon was terrified, and she could see the flames in Bernice's eyes.

Cinnamon could sense that something painful was about to take place. Bernice double slapped Cinnamon so hard across the face that she left her hand print on the left side of Cinnamons cheeks. She picked Cinnamon's little body up by her throat and threw her on the top shelf of the closet located in the hallway. She then slammed the door shut, then yelled, "You're never coming out Red bitch".

Cinnamon screamed and yelled for hours, "Please let me out, I'm so sorry!". Sadly her pleading and crying was ignored. She tilted her head towards the floor, and instantly became terrified of how high up she was from the floor. Her little body began to tremble with fear until something miraculously happened; Cinnamon was greeted with this angelic presence. This godly spirit held her in its arms and told her that it will always protect and comfort her through her journey in this demonic world.

Cinnamon felt a feeling of peace and calmness before drifting off to sleep. Six hours went by before Bernice decided to let Cinnamon out of the closet.

Their aunts were cruel and evil, but the uncles seemed to be okay—especially Uncle Girt who was twenty-two years old and stood about six feet, three inches and he weighed about 205 pounds. He was cool, or so the kids thought. He basically allowed the children to do whatever they wanted to do because he was so busy getting high.

He was an addict, thief, gangster, and a pimp. He had a girlfriend named Sierra and another girlfriend named Mini. Both the women knew about each other

and both of them got pregnant at the same time, which meant that Girt had two daughters in the same year. Cinnamon once witnessed Girt, and the both of Girt girlfriends laying in the bed naked together.

It was the summer of 1991, and Sierra was pregnant. Mona was fed up with Girt, the stealing and lying was becoming too much for her to handle. Mona was at the end of her ropes, so she kicked Girt and his women Sierra out of the apartment which resulted in Girt becoming homeless. One afternoon, Cinnamon was playing in the hallway with her best friend Maria when Bernice yelled for her to come inside for dinner. Cinnamon being Cinnamon ignored Bernice; she hated the way Bernice cooked, it was disgusting.

Girt came out of nowhere staggering off of the elevator, high as a kite. When he noticed Cinnamon and Maria playing in the hallway he slowly leaned against the wall. As they ran up and down the hallway, Girt lustfully watched Cinnamon and slowly began to get an erection. Maria's front door opens as her father slightly tilts his head out the door to call her name "Maria!!" he calmly yelled. "Si, Papi," said Maria as she ran to go to see what her father wanted. As she walked into the apartment, the door slam shut behind her. "Bye, Maria " Cinnamon sadly mumbles while waving goodbye and running over to Girt.

Ever since Mona kicked out Girt and one of his pregnant girl-friends Cinnamon wanted to find out where the baby will live. Uncle Girt, where are you Ciara and the baby going to live?" She asked while looking up at Girt with her big, brown eyes.

"Come on let me show you," he said in a smooth seductive tone. He lick his lips then turns around to walk towards the elevators. Cinnamon followed behind him and entered the elevator. She would rather go with him then to be in the house dealing with Bernice craziness. Besides that Girt was her favorite uncle and she trust him. As they entered the elevator, it was drenched of beer and cigarette smoke. They reached the lower lobby, and Girt held Cinnamon's hand and lead her to the back stairway. He pushed the door opened before saying "This is where I live, this is where the baby will live when she is born, go take a look" .Cinnamon curiously walked inside the stairway and was confused at what she saw. NOTHING. She instantly became confused and turned around to see if Girt was joking. Girt gave her a sexually seductive look while slowly removing his shirt. He nearly placed his shirt on the cold concrete floor.

"Let me show you how we sleep," Girt said as he rubbed on her little behind while sliding off her pink flower shorts. As he started to remove her shirt this young guy was walking down the steps toward the exit and instantly stopped."Ooh, I'm so sorry" he nervously said. The guy appeared to be Hispanic; he was tall with a mustache and had a head full of curly hair.

By the looks of his khaki pants and navy blue shirt that had the NYCHA logo written on it, one would assume that he was the main-tenance guy. Girt quickly kicked the shirt to the side as fast as he could and said, "Oh, I just brought her down here to pee because we are locked out of the house."

"Oh ok, I understand," said the Hispanic guy, oblivious to the fact that Cinnamon had a look on her face that said, "Help me, he's lying!!" But instead, the guy turned around and walked away.

Girt reached over to the left of him, grabbed his t-shirt, and neatly laid it on the cold concrete floor.

Girt slowly laid Cinnamon on the top of his dingy off white t-shirt..

He then kneeled down, pulled out his penis and began to rub it against Cinnamon's vagina. Cinnamon entered a state of shock, and her body was completely stuck. Moaning and groaning Girt kissed her on her cheeks, and asked her if she liked it. Confused, not knowing how to reply, Cinnamon replied,"Yes, I do," .

She couldn't believe what Girt was doing to her, she trusted him; he was her safety net; he was the only one who seemed to truly care about her.

After he was done doing what he was doing, he ejaculated all over her legs and thighs.

Breathing heavily without a conscience, Girt quickly stood up, pulled up his pants, and zipped up his zipper.

He lifted Cinnamons little body up and fixed her clothing as fast as he could.

Cinnamon was emotionally numb when realizing that her vaginal area didn't feel normal; it felt sore.

"Go upstairs, and if anybody asks you where you were, tell them that I took you to the park," is what Girt told her as he quickly walked her to the elevator. Girt was high out of his mind, and ran out of the building as fast as he could.

Before Cinnamon could get a chance to knock on the door, her aunt Bernice swung the door open. "Where the hell have you been ? We've been looking all over for you! Get in here Red Hefa!" her Aunt aggressively demanded, after slapping Cinnamon as hard as she could across her face.

While walking into the house, Bernice noticed that Cinnamon was walking weird. She looked down at Cinnamon's little five-year-old frame and couldn't help but notice this thick white fluid on her legs that was semi-dry but not fully.

Bernice also noticed that Cinnamon's shorts were turnt inside out.

"Come here girl and sit your ass on the couch "What is this on your legs?" she suspiciously asked at the same time pointing at Cinnamon's upper left leg.

Cinnamon who looked as if her heart had been ripped out nodded her shoulders to imply that she didn't know. "Where were you, and who were you with?" Bernice suspiciously asked.

Cinnamon was terrified of what would happen if she lied to Bernice. Sadly Cinnamon held her head down before she morosely whispered "I was with Uncle Girt". "Where did y'all go?" Bernice nervously asked terrified of the answer Cinnamon was about to give her.

Cinnamon spilled her guts; she could not and would not lie to Bernice about have just taken place.

Bernice was in shock about all of what she had just heard. "Oh, my Jesus," is all that she could say.

"Auntie, it hurts when I try to close my legs," Cinnamon painfully uttered while realizing her uncle Teddy was standing in the hallway listening to what she was telling Bernice.

Teddy furiously walked to his closet to grab his pistol and left the house in a rage. Bernice ran after him trying to convince him to not kill Girt but uncle Teddy wasn't trying to hear it. Instead he gave Bernice a look that said "Girl do you want some of this shit too!". She knew that looked all too well, before she knew it she found herself backing the hell up, and she did it fast.

Teddy wanted Girt to pay for what he did to Cinnamon. He WANTED GIRT DEAD!!!

He searched the neighborhood for hours; he even asked the local crackheads and drug dealers if they seen him but had no luck. Girt was in hiding, and stayed away for about six weeks.

When he came back around, everybody acted like nothing happened. Cinnamon was not taken to the doctor nor was she taken to a psychologist. Mona felt as though it was best to not involve the police. She didn't want her son to go to jail, so everything was swept under the rug.

That was the first time Girt molested Cinnamon, but it definitely wasn't the last. Cinnamon's innocence was taken at the age of five and didn't stop until a year later when Girt was murdered in Castle Hill projects.

He was stabbed by his girlfriend's step-dad when he went over to his girlfriend's house to beat her ass for not bringing him his money after she sucked another man's dick. His girlfriend lived with her mom and step dad in the project building across the street from Mona.

Girt was banging on his girlfriend's door demanding her to open the door. Fearful of what Girt would do if she didn't oblige, she unlocked the door, opened it and got a fist to the face.

Noticing blood gushing from her daughter's nose Girt 's girlfriend's mother started cursing him out, which resulted in Girt slapping the tastes out of her mouth. Girts girlfriend's stepfather decided to intervene. Girt beat his ass like a runaway slave, but the step father refused to lose. Girt gave the stepfather an uppercut to the jaw and turned around so he could continue beating his girlfriend's ass. The stepfather staggered into the kitchen, grabbed a knife. While Girt's back was turnt he continuously stabbed Girt six times in his back. Girt slowly drifted out of the apartment towards the staircase. He made it to the stairway exit, but couldn't continue any further.

Teddy was the one who found him in the staircase dead; the cause of death was caused by Grit drowning in his own blood. In addition to all of that Cinnamon thought Girts death would be the end of the molestation, but oh was she wrong.

One day Cinnamon and her cousins were sitting in the living room watching cartoons. Mona, Bernice and uncle Teddy were out doing only God knows what. Uncle Roy was babysitting that day, he appeared to be higher than a kite and extremely intoxicated.

He looked like he had not slept in weeks as he continually paced around the house, mumbling obscene words to himself. "Fucked this shit; I'm going to show them motherfuckers, I'm that Nigga in these projects." Is what his crazy ass was saying.

For some reason, every time he got high, he thought that he was some type of gangster, but in reality, he was the scariest Nigga around. "Fuck that shit. I'm gonna show these motherfuckers," he said to himself as he slammed the door as he exited the apartment, which was the fifth time he had left the kids alone.

He returned about thirty minutes later, eyes bucked open like an owl. "Come here, girl," said Roy as he pointed to Cinnamon.

"Do you want some candy?" he asked. "Yeah," Cinnamon replied. Roy walked into the hallway of the apartment which had a closet door in the center.

If the closet door was open and you looked down the hallway, no one would be able to tell who was in the closet or hallway.

He stood inside the closet, pulled his penis out and told her to open her mouth. Roy slowly inserted his penis in and out of her mouth. Afterwards he demanding Cinnamon to follow him into the bathroom. He laid her down on the floor and then asked,

"Where do you want me to put it?" he points at her vagina and asks, "Or do you want it in the back?" From experience Cinnamon knew how painful it would be from the back, so she pointed to the front.

Cinnamon laid there helplessly until he was done. He walked out of the bathroom into the kitchen and reached on top of the refrigerator to grab her a honey bun. Roy looked at her and said, "You better never tell anyone what just happened." She shook her head up and down to imply that she wouldn't say a word. Why would she? It's not like something would be done about it.

Cinnamon skipped towards the living room to watch cartoons. Her cousins seemed as though they were in their own world; they seemed oblivious to what was going on. "How did you get a snack, and we didn't get one?" One Cinnamon's cousin curiously asked.

"Uncle Roy!!" the cousin yelled, "How come Cinnamon got a honey bun, but we didn't?" she asked. He then replied, "Cinnamon earned it. Maybe, one day, you will earn it the same way she did," he stated with a devilish look in his eyes.

Cinnamon had never seen Roy with a girlfriend until this lady and a six month old baby boy from Mississippi came to New York to visit Roy. She and her baby Roy Jr. stayed with Mona for about three months.

His baby's mother had a weird feeling about Roy because, on a particular rainy day, she pulled Cinnamon to the side when nobody was around, and asked if Roy had ever touched her in her private area.

Cinnamon was caught off guard by the question. "I need you to tell me the truth, honey," she said in a more serious tone. Cinnamon hesitated for a second; she figured why tell the truth nobody cares anyways.

"No ma'am. Uncle Roy has never touched me in my private area," said Cinnamon. "Are you sure baby?" she asked, not really believing what Cinnamon was telling her. "Yes, I'm sure, '' Cinnamon said in her shy little girl voice. Roy's baby's mother looked down at Cinnamon and said, "I'm here for you if you need me. Now go ahead to the living room and watch TV."

Roy's baby's mother was originally from Mississippi. He had convinced her to leave her family and move to New York City. Roy's baby mother always had this feeling of suspense when it came to Roy and the way he would undress Cinnamon with his eyes.

One day, Roy's baby mother walked into the bedroom where Cinnamon was sound asleep in bed. When Roy's baby mother walked in, she witnessed Roy's hands inside of Cinnamon's shorts.

When Roy noticed his baby mother walking into the room, he acted as if he was checking to see if she had wet the bed.

Roy's baby mother knew about his brother Girt and how he liked to touch little girls, she definitely didn't put it past Roy to be a child molester as well.

A month later, Roy's baby mother decided to go back to Mississippi, the City life was not for her. Plus, Roy's addiction was becoming out of control, and she didn't want Roy. Jr to be in that type of environment.

Cinnamon wished she could have gone with them; she often daydreamed about moving away with someone who loved her unconditionally, and someonewho cared about her well-being.

She was a six-year-old girl who didn't know what it felt like to be wanted, loved, or liked. It was over a decade before she opened up and told anyone about what Roy had done to her.

CHAPTER 2

VIRGINIA

Everything seemed to be piling up on Mona. Her children were on drugs, she lost her son, her grandkids were being molested, and her daughters were both pregnant. At the same time, her kids were disrespecting her to the fullest. She came to the conclusion that she had to get her and her grandkids out of the projects for good, and away from her demonic children.

She found a three-bedroom apartment on the other side of the Bronx. Cinnamon, Lil' Virginia, and Tavon loved it.

Eventually, their Uncle Teddy moved in; he was a mama's boy. It seemed as though he was never going to move from up under Mona's shadow. Teddy was her favorite and vice-versa.

The move was a great deal for everyone, and everything seemed to be coming together, except for one thing. Cinnamon was missing something; she was missing the love, care, and affection of her mother who she hadn't seen in five years.

No visit, no calls, nothing which resulted in Cinnamon feeling like she had done something wrong, like she wasn't worth her mother's time.

Cinnamon thought she was not good enough for her mother. She couldn't make herself understand why her mother didn't love her enough to pick up the phone to call or visit. How could a mother not love her child? Is the question that stayed on Cinnamon's mind.

One afternoon Mona sat on the couch gossiping on the phone as she normally did. This particular gossip was about Virginia. "Word around town was that Virginia was seen in Harlem!!!??, and pushing a baby girl in a stroller?" Mona asked in extreme shock.

Cinnamon crept up behind her grandmother after eavesdropping on the conversation for about five minutes.

At age seven, Cinnamon was a very smart and intellectual. "Did I hear you talking on the phone about my mother? Is it true that I have a little sister? Well, is it true, Ma. Is it true?" Cinnamon excitedly asked as she jumped up and down.

Mona looked down at Cinnamon's pretty little face, and then, held her head down before responding, "Yes, it's true. You got a baby sister; isn't that something?" Mona asked as she got up to walk to her room to finish her conversation. After the phone call Mona felt disgusted with Virginia. She thought that Virginia was wrong to raise another baby without trying to get full custody of her kids.

Mona walked out of her room to where Cinnamon was. "Don't worry, baby. We are going to find her or die trying," Mona said to Cinnamon as she looked down at her big, brown eyes, meaning every single word.

The next day, Mona decided to spend the whole day investigating the location of her daughter Virginia. First step was to make a few phone calls.

"Hello, how are you?"

I'm okay. Who is this?" asked the young lady on the other end of the phone, who sounded a little puzzled because she really couldn't catch the voice that was on the other end of the phone.

"This is Mona Stalks, stop playing, April!!" Mona yelled. "Oh, LOL. Hi, stranger!!" How are you girl?" stated April "I'm okay, girl.

Just hanging in there, taking care of these grandchildren of mine," said Mona.

Mona didn't waste any time and decided to get straight to the point, "Well, speaking of these grandchildren of mine," she said, "I was told that you ran into Virginia in Harlem, and she was pushing a stroller." Mona humbly stated.

"I was leaving the supermarket on 132nd St. and St. Nicholas, and on my way out, I looked across the street and saw Virginia pushing a purple stroller.

She was moving kind of fast when I called out for her, so I ran across the street. We greeted each other and that's when she told me that she just moved into a brand-new building not too far from the Bronx zoo." April stated.

Mona was shocked; it seemed as though she wanted it to be untrue. What kind of mother would abandon their kids then go out and have another one.

"Well, did she ask about her kids?" asked Mona. "No, after she told me about the apartment, she said she had to take the baby to an doctors appointment and told me it was nice seeing me and walked away." "Well, I'll be damned. What type of bullshit is that?" said Mona, "this woman got me raising her damn kids and has the audacity to have another one like these kids don't need their mother."

"I really do appreciate you, and thanks a lot, April," Mona said as she slammed the phone down. She sent the kids to school the following day, and decided to skip work. She was not going to rest until she found Virginia. The plan was to ride the 19 Bus to Southern Boulevard.

That's exactly what she did; she arrived at her destination. It was a nice day, so Mona figured that she would run into Virginia eventually. She sat patiently on a bench, at the park that was on the boulevard.

One hour went by, then two, then three but there was no sign of Virginia. Mona was so anxious that she forgot to eat something for breakfast. Her stomach was growling so bad that if anyone was to walk by, they could hear it.

I'm starving, she thought to herself. Mona was faced with a dilemma to either get something to eat and miss bumping into Virginia, or sit there and be hungry and patient.

Her stomach was growling and didn't agree with her staying there hungry, so she quickly made the decision to get something to eat. She walked two blocks down the street to this Chinese restaurant. Soon as she walked in, the aroma of fried chicken smacked her in her face.

"Yes, how can I help you?" asked this short Chinese girl who looked like she was ten years old. "Well, let me get the Number 6 with a Sprite. Also, I need to ask you a question. Do you know a lady by the name of Virginia?" Before she could finish the rest of the question, Virginia walked into the Chinese restaurant with the same purple stroller April was telling her about.

The baby was so adorable she had these cute little box braids with colorful beads that match her outfit.She was a calm happy baby and clean from head to toe. Mona was amazed at how well this little girl was taking care of. Mona was ecstatic that her dedication and patience had paid off.

All of Mona's children were grown, and she loved her grandchildren to death, but would rather be a grandmother instead. When Virginia walked into the Chinese restaurant, her mouth dropped to her feet. The last person she wanted to see was her mother—"THE MISS MONA STALKS".

The last time she had seen Mona, she was told that she was a bad mother who chose drugs over her children. Virginia felt as though she was the black sheep of the family; she felt like her mother had hated her for as long as she could remember. As a child Virginia spent a lot of time in church alongside with her grandmother who raised her. Virginia dreamed of becoming a Nun; her love for God was extremely high.

Nothing good ever came out of Mona's mouth when it came to Virginia. Let me rephrase that, nothing good came out of Mona's mouth when it came to anyone. Virginia couldn't understand that Miss Mona didn't hate her; she just wanted her to get herself together, if not for herself then for her children. When Virginia laid eyes on her mother, she tried to turn around and run as fast as she could, but her feet wouldn't move, she was stuck physically and mentally. Since Virginia was standing there looking like a deer in headlights, Mona took it upon herself to break the ice. "What's up, girl? Where the hell have you been hiding?" Mona sarcastically asked.

"How the hell did you find me?" Virginia asked with the nastiest attitude.

"Don't worry about that, that's unimportant," said Mona, "what matters is that your children need you; they haven't seen their mother in five fucking years, and that's a damn shame." Mona looked Virginia directly in her eyes and told her that she was a sorry excuse for a mother.

Virginia didn't say a word, and as much as she would have hate to admit it, she knew that Mona was telling the truth. At the same time Virginia felt like who the fuck made Mona mother of the year it's not she raised any of her damn children. When it all was said and done Mona wasn't no better than Virginia when it came to being a mother.

Mona was the type to tell you what was on her mind, no matter if you liked it or not.

Mona looked Virginia in her eyes as she sat down at the table.

"I didn't mean to start off with this negative attitude. Truth be told your kids miss you, and we need to come up with a plan to get you in your kids' lives. How do you feel about them spending the weekends with you?7 They can get on 19 Bus straight here."

"I guess that's fine," Virginia said in an uncertain voice, but deep down inside this is what Virginia has been praying for.

They sat there and talked for the next hour, afterwards Virginia showed Mona exactly where she lived. They Exchanged numbers and went their separate ways.

The following Friday Cinnamon, Lil'Virginia and Tavon were on the bus to spend the weekend with their mother.

The hole that was planted in their hearts by abandonment seemed to be filled with love and joy.

Virginia met the kids at the bus stop—she and her baby girl Chassidy. Cinnamon was ecstatic to have a cute little sister. Definitely happy to be in the presence of her mother. The times the kids spent with Virginia were priceless. They would make homemade popcorn with ice water and watch movies all day. Virginia loved her movies and puzzle books.

When it was really hot, they would walk to the park down the block and spend the whole day at the park, having the best time of their life; if it wasn't the park, they would go to the Bronx Zoo.

Virginia made Cinnamon feel like a person like a human being. She wasn't being sexually and physically abused when she was with her mom. She wished that she could live the rest of her life with her mother.

Virginia on the other hand was trying to process the fact that Mona actually found her. Virginia never intended on seeing her children because of the evil spirit that lied within Mona.

Virginia fantasized about how it would have been to have a loving relationship with her mother. never had a mother.

Her father was a married man who fornicated with Mona.

When his wife found out about his infidelity with Mona, she insisted that they pack up, leave Mississippi,and move to Milwaukee before Virginia was born..

Virginia didn't really want anything to do with Mona; since the kids were in her custody, she didn't want much to do with them as well. The reason being that she knew Mona brain washed them into thinking Virginia was a horrible person.

Mona couldn't convince Cinnamon that her mother was pitiful. Mona was strict when it came to Cinnamon because she saw too much of Virginia in her.

One night, Mona had a nightmare that Cinnamon was prostituting her body for crack, and went down the same path as Virginia. She felt that Cinnamon was becoming too promiscuous and needed a change of location. After a few years of going to spend time with her mother on weekends,

Cinnamon got the worst news ever.

Mona decided to move the kids and herself down south. The city life was becoming too much for her. She wanted to be somewhere quite warm and slow. Cinnamon was devastated; she didn't want to be disconnected from her mother yet again.

She started acting out in school, every day she was getting into trouble. Her fourth-grade year was the year she started to resent Mona for taking her away from her mother; she felt like nobody gave a fuck about what she wanted or how she felt, so why the hell should she?

CHAPTER 3

SUICIDE

They left New York City for good, and Virginia did nothing to show her kids that she wanted them to stay. No tears were shed nor were there any goodbyes. It seemed as if she didn't give a damn if they stayed or left.

Cinnamon seemed to be the one who was the most upset. Her mother, whom she adored, was out of her life yet again.

Mona and uncle Teddy took turns driving the long drive to Mississippi.

Upon arrival they pulled up in a trailer park which was a lot different from what Cinnamon Lil Virginia and Tavon were used to. What amazed them was the quietness and the freshness of the air.

"Alright, now get your butt in this house and unpack those boxes," yelled Mona as she and the kids exited the vehicle. Cinnamon decided she wanted to get smart.

"This ain't no house, it's a nasty old trailer," she said.

Mona wanted to curse the little heifer out, but decided to get that ass later.

"That damn girl is going to make me hurt her! I don't know what got into that girl, she's changing" Kay," said Mona.

Kay was Mona's little sister who actually helped Mona get into the trailer park. Kay resided at the trailer park as well along with her four grandchildren.

Kay was in the same situation as Mona so much so that she had full custody of all four of her grandchildren, and for the same exact reason. Kay's daughter was an addict, her main focus was finding her next fix.

Next thing you know, they heard a big boom. "Get off her," Tavon yelled at the top of his lungs. Kay and Mona rushed into the trailer as fast as they could. When they made it inside the house, Cinnamon was on top of little Virginia, choking the hell out of her.

"What the hell has gotten into you, child?" Mona yelled as she lifted Cinnamon up off Lil Virginia by her shirt.

"Calm your ass down Cinnamon, what the hell has gotten into you?" yelled Mona. "I hate it here, I hate everybody! I wanna go back to New York with my mother!!" Cinnamon shouted.

Mona lost it, she couldn't hold back the truth anymore, "If your mother wanted you, don't you think you would be with her, you dummy!? Your mother doesn't want you!! Why do you think you are with me?" Mona shouted . Those words penetrated through Cinnamon's heart like a knife.

Her eyes filled with tears as she tearfully yelled, "That's not true!!!!My mother loves us!!!!. I don't believe you!!" She then ran off into the bathroom and slammed the door shut behind her. Cinnamon sat on the toilet seat rocking back and forth while repeatedly saying, "I hate my life; I just want to die."

Cinnamon felt worthless and unloved and strangely started to hear voices in her head. She was only eleven, and she was trying to figure out a way to commit suicide.

She looked over to her left and noticed that there was a pair of scissors sitting near the sink. A quiet voice came over saying, "Nobody loves you, nobody wants you. Just grab the scissors and push it into your stomach. You'll feel better, you won't have to deal with what's going on."

Cinnamon took the scissors, closed her eyes, and pressed it against her stomach. That voice appeared again and it whispered, "Yea that's right, press it harder."

She pressed it harder, so hard that it started to pierce through her skin, and bleed. "Ouch," Cinnamon said while at the same time, accidentally dropping the scissors on the floor. She then started to cry; she cried because her mother was not in her life once again; she cried because she didn't like being down south; she cried because of what her uncles did to her. She cried because nobody asked her how she felt about being molested; she cried because nobody cared. She sat on the toilet and cried her little heart out until someone decided to interrupt her crying by banging on the bathroom door. "Boom boom boom boom" Cinnamon yelled at whoever it was knocking on the door. "What do you want? Leave me alone!!" She screamed

"It's me, girl, open the damn door!!" yelled Mona, as she felt frustrated that she had to wait so damn long to get into her own bathroom.

Cinnamon was startled; she didn't want Mona to see her in the state that she was in. "Okay, Ma," she calmly said while splashing some cold water on her face.

She turned the water on then off as if she was about to wash her hands. Then she opened the bathroom door and ran past Mona as fast as she could. Mona stood there in confusion as Cinnamon ran past her like a crazy person. *I don't know what to say about that girl sometimes*, she thought to herself.

Then all of a sudden, she heard a door slam shut. It was Cinnamon once again. She ran into the bedroom and kneeled down in front of the window and began to pray. "God, I hate it here. I want to be with my mother, please God. I will do what it is that you want me to do, I swear." Her strong faith came from her spiritual connection that day when she was thrown into the closet by her aunt for the first time. Her mother would talk about God so much so that it stuck with Cinnamon.

After praying, Cinnamon went into Mona's room without being noticed and grabbed a bunch of pill bottles out of Mona's makeup bag. She went into her room, grabbed the glass of water off her dresser and swallowed over 30 pills.

Fifteen minutes later, she was unconscious for almost three days. It was difficult for her to get out of bed to use the restroom during those three days but she miraculously did it.

When the drowsiness finally wore off , she was upset because she was still alive. She was also upset that God had not taken her life.

The following week, after eating breakfast, Mona went into her bedroom to take her meds.

When she reached into her bag with her pills in it, she noticed that some of her meds were missing.

"I know it wasn't nobody else but Cinnamon, who else would be going through my pills!" I know she didn't throw away my medicine, she got to go!!" Mona furiously stated to herself. Little did she know that Cinnamon didn't throw away her pills, actually she swallowed every single one. ."Cinnamon!!!!!" Mona yelled as loud as she could.

"Come here, girl." Cinnamon walked in the room with little shorts, a red tank top shirt, red lipstick, and some red flip-flops.

"Why in the world would you throw away my damn pills?" she asked. Cinnamon's eyes opened wide like a deer in headlights. "Well, answer me!" yelled Mona. Cinnamon opened her mouth, but her words wouldn't come out, so she just stood there, looking stupid.

She wanted to tell Mona that she didn't throw her pills away, she swallowed them because she wanted to die.

She also wanted to tell her how much she hated it down south, that she misses her mother. She wanted to tell her how much she felt alone and unwanted, how she just wanted to die, but those words never left her mouth.

"Girl, get out of here; I can't stand to look at your nasty ass right now," said Miss Mona. Afterwards Mona spent the whole day trying to figure out what she was going to do about Cinnamon. Her behavior was becoming unbearable. Mona had to worry about the other four kids in the house.

A while back after Girt got murdered when Mona moved from Castle Hill Projects she gained custody of Girts's son and daughter. Girt's baby mother gave up her parental rights after her stepfather murdered Girt.

She couldn't stand the guilt of it all and sign over custody of her children to Mona.

That night, Mona stayed up all night trying to find a solution to the dilemma she was facing. She had to face the reality that Cinnamon was becoming a major problem. She felt that she had no choice but to send Cinnamon back to her mother. The last thing she wanted

was for Cinnamon reckless behavior to rub off on the other kids. Her mind was made up; she was sending her back to New York to live with her mother, whether it was a good decision or not, Mona really didn't care.

Cinnamon had to leave point blank simple. Meanwhile, Cinnamon was in the next room on her knees praying as she normally did every night for the same thing as usual. "Dear God, I will do anything you want if you only make it possible for me to live with my mother."

Her mother always talked to her and her siblings about the spiritual world. She would preach from time to time about how God was a merciful God. Virginia told them that if you had a good heart and good intentions, good things will follow. Mona never took them to church, never had discussion about Heaven or Hell. After praying, she got into bed, pulled the covers over herself and fell asleep. Months went by, and before you knew it, school was about to end and summer was near. Mona decided that every summer the kids would go stay with Virginia in New York. She let it be known loud and clear that

Cinnamon would not be coming back. The other kids would come back to continue school in Mississippi.

Cinnamon was excited that her prayers were finally answered. She will be with the person she loved most, the one and only person she loved more than any one. The only person in this world she cared about.

She felt as though life would be so much better if she was with her mother. She knew for a fact that she would be treated with respect. She knew that being with her mother was the best place for her … or so she thought.

Meanwhile Mona, on the other hand, knew what might become of Cinnamon. She was a hundred percent okay with the decision that she had made by sending Cinnamon off to live with her mother, but there was a feeling that she might have made the wrong choice by doing so.

Mona waved goodbye to the kids as the Greyhound Bus slowly left the service station. She humbly wished Cinnamon the best; she was no longer her concern.

CHAPTER 4

THE BIG APPLE

New York City was amazing and Cinnamon loved it there. Summer went by so quickly, two months flew by like a bird in the sky, and before you knew it, the kids were off to Mississippi except Cinnamon. She was happy to be staying for good. She had been praying to God for so long, and God finally answered her prayers. The entire summer was like a routine between the pool and free lunch. Virginia couldn't afford to feed everyone, so she forced the kids to to go to the five schools in the area that fed the community children free breakfast and lunch between mom-fri.

In Cinnamon's mind, the move was the happiest moment in her life thus far. She knew for a fact that anything beats living with her judgmental grandmother.

When Cinnamon would visit Virginia on weekends, she had a few friends she would hang out with in the neighborhood park.

She soon found out that she would be attending the same school as her friends from the neighborhood. The following Monday after the kids left New York Virginia took Cinnamon to the school down the block for registration. As soon as Cinnamon and her mother arrived at the school, Cinnamon noticed a few familiar faces.

"Hey, Cinnamon," one girl with two pony tails said, as she smiled and waved. All Cinnamon could do was smile and wave back. After finishing up the paperwork for registration the vice principal informed Virginia that Cinnamon would start school the following day.

That Tuesday morning Cinnamon woke up earlier than she should have, she was so excited to be attending school that she was one of the first kids to arrive.

Once she located her class room, she slowly walked inside. The first face she noticed was this girl from the neighborhood named Mandy, she decided to sit in the empty desk next to her. "What's up, girl!" Cinnamon said with a big smile on her face.

"Hey, Cinnamon!" Said Mandy, "we've been missing you bitch. Where the hell have you been?"

"Down south, and I hated it with a passion," said Cinnamon. Cinnamon was in the fifth grade, but she thought she was in ninth grade, and in her mind, she thought she was a grown woman. Cinnamon seem to adapt well, and she made sure her peers treated her with respect. Her thoughts were that she would not tolerate people treating her like her family treated her.

The library was the hangout spot for the fifth graders. It was located about two blocks away from the elementary school.

Around this time the Internet wasn't as popular as it is now. The public library was the main source of information. Cinnamon and her Friends from school would spend at least two hours at the library.

One beautiful sunny day after school Cinnamon walked into the library with Mandy and another girl. They decided to sit at the table next to a girl named Jessica. Jessica was the girl everyone stayed away from because they thought she was crazy. Honestly that never seemed to bother Jessica; she really didn't care what the kids at school thought about her.

She was always by herself with an expression on her face that said " 'Fuck the world.' It was something about Jessica that Cinnamon liked, but she couldn't pinpoint it.

Jessica was a tough girl who was raised by a woman that didn't put up with any bullshit. She was the second to the oldest and had a sibling under her. Her mother was outspoken and aggressive, especially when it came to disciplining her children. She believed in the old saying "Spare the rod, spoil the child." Trust me, the rod she did not spare, LOL.

One day after school, the girls met up at the library as usual. Mandy and the girls were gossiping about Jessica when Cinnamon walked up to the table. "She thinks she's hard with her dusty ass," said one of the girls.

"Who are y'all bitches talking about now?" asked Cinnamon as she plunged into the chair next to the girls.

Mandy held her two fingers over her nose as she turned and pointed to Jessica, "Fuck her I will beat that bitch ass!!!.

As a matter of fact, I don't like her, and I want to fight her" said Cinnamon as she stood up out of her seat. Mandy, go tell her to meet me outside in front of the library in 10 minutes," Cinnamon aggressively stated. "You ain't gotta tell me twice," Mandy said while jumping up and walking over Jessica. "Cinnamon wants to fight you, so meet her outside in ten minutes," Mandy said to Jessica as she held her fingers to her nose to imply that Jessica hygiene was off.

Jessica sat there with her I-don't-give-a-fuck look on her face. Mandy then walked back to the table to where Cinnamon was. Mandy was excited that she was gonna get to see Cinnamon best Jessica's ass.

Ten minutes went by when Cinnamon and the girls started to head outside to get it popping.

Like three minutes later, Jessica came walking out of the library in a nonchalant manner. Her attitude and body language said "Whatever, let's do this; let's get this shit over with."

"Take your book bag off bitch," said Cinnamon, as she took her book bag off and dropped it on the floor. Unsuspectingly, Jessica's mom walked up two seconds later "What's going on, Jessica?" she asked, even though she had an idea of what was about to take place because of the number of kids that circled around Jessica and Cinnamon.

"I don't know, Ma; they told me to come outside because they wanted to fight," Jessica said to her mother. "Oh really," said her mom, "well, you can either stay here and fight or go with me, but it's up to you." Jessica looked at Cinnamon, and then, she looked at her mom.

While looking Cinnamon in her eyes, she said, "I'm staying." "Okay, I will see you at home, Baby," Jessica's mom said as she proceeded to walk home.

Cinnamon was speechless and surprised, but at the same time, she respected the fact that Jessica stood her ground. At that very moment Cinnamon decided that she would rather have Jessica in her circle." *She's fearless, and I love it!"* Cinnamon thought to herself. Cinnamon glanced at the crowd of kids before saying . "I have better things to do".

She then grabbed her book bag and walked away from the crowd.

Jessica slowly reached down, snatched her book bag off the ground, and calmly walked in the opposite direction of Cinnamon.

The following day at school Cinnamon spotted Jessica sitting on the right side of the cafeteria eating lunch. Filled with confidence she walked over in that direction. Jessica was sitting next to a girl name was Janae. She was really cute with pretty long hair.

She always had a smile on her face and everyone seemed to love her. Cinnamon rolled her eyes and walked right past Janae. "What's up?" Cinnamon said to Jessica while giving her a big smile. "I just wanted to apologize about what happened yesterday at the library. I can be a bully when I want to be," Cinnamon told her, while looking straight in her eyes and waiting for a response. "It's all good," said Jessica. For some reason, Jessica liked the way Cinnamon carried herself. The fact that she was carefree and lived life on the edge was an automatic attraction for Jessica.

They sat there laughing and chatting until it was time to return back to their class room.

From that day forward, they became best friends. If you saw Cinnamon, Jessica wasn't too far behind. They ended up terrorizing junior high school together, fighting and getting suspended was the norm for the two girls. Janae was with them too, but she was the quiet type. She was strong minded so she really didn't follow after Cinnamon and Jessica when they would do wild and crazy things.

Janae was raised a little different from Cinnamon and Jessica. She didn't endure so much of the verbal and physical abuse that they endured. Instead of getting beaten, when she got in trouble, her mother would put her on punishment.

Punishments seemed to work because Janae hated not being able to go outside, so she would do everything it took to not get into any kind of trouble. Despite their differences, the three seemed to hit it off very well, and they were inseparable.

The song *"Ruff Ryders Anthem"* by DMX and the Ruff Ryders took over the music game like crazy. Everywhere throughout the city, people were blasting music by the rapper DMX. Cinnamon, Jessica and Janae enjoyed themselves every time they were together,.the streets was exciting to them, they loved every bit of it.

Meanwhile Cinnamon thought life with Virginia would be a dream come true,but instead it was the opposite.

Virginia was still using drugs, and it affected the way that her house was run. Virginia would come home and verbally abuse Cinnamon every time she got high off drugs.

Chastity's father lived with them from time to time, better yet he was there until Virginia occasionally kicked his ass out."What the hell are you doing in my house with my damn man?" Virginia viscously asked as she staggered into the house drunk and high as a kite.

Cinnamon looked at her mother as if she lost her damn mind before replying "Nothing, just sitting here watching TV."

"Well, take your nasty ass in the room because only God knows what you've been doing with my damn man." Virginia aggressively told her as glanced at her baby father who was laying on a dusty mattress placed in the center of the living room . The way she talked to Cinnamon you would think that she was speaking to a bitch on the streets.

Cinnamon held her head down as she stood up and walked into the bedroom with her baby sister. There was no TV in the bedroom which was the only reason why she was in the living room.

Cinnamon laid her ass beside her sister until she eventually drifted off to sleep.

The following morning Cinnamon woke up thinking about how she was going to get the fuck up out of the house. Getting away from the house has been Cinnamon's daily routine. Every chance she got, she would try to be as far away from Virginia as possible.

Cinnamon could not stand the way her mother would downgrade her and verbally abuse her. She couldn't help but to think that Virginia was jealous of her.

Virginia didn't buy her any school clothes, underwear, shoes, nothing. She would wear the same sneakers and clothes for years.

The only thing Virginia did was make sure Cinnamon didn't starve to death.

When Cinnamon entered high school, the majority of the students was there to make a fashion statement .

You had the cool kids who were dressed to kill, you had the nerds who sat at the lunch table playing chess, and you had the Gothic weirdos who listened to heavy-metal music and wore all-black.

Then you had Cinnamon, the one who couldn't afford to dress to impress because her mother spent up every dime she had on drugs.

She wasn't intelligent enough to chill with the nerds who played chess. She didn't give a damn if she wasn't weird enough to chill with the Gothics because she wasn't trying to hang out with them mutha fuckers anyways.

Cinnamon decided that she was going to be down with whoever the fuck she wanted to be down with, the ones that dress to impress. She made the decision to be a fly bitch.

All of this took place around the time Cinnamon reconnected with her father.

One night Cinnamon and Virginia got into a heated argument.

Virginia kicked her out of the house, and told her not to bring her ass back.

Since her father ain't never do shit for her, Cinnamon moved in with him and his wife. Her father and his wife were foreigners originally from Guatemala. When her dad was fourteen he arrive in the United States illegally.

The issue with her dad is that he was cheap as fuck.

For example, Cinnamon asked for a pair of sneakers he bought her a $20 pair of sneakers from a street vendor. She never wore the sneakers, instead she gave them

away to a family member who mentioned something about those sneakers being one of the best sneakers she ever had.

Enough was enough in Cinnamon's mind, she was going to give herself a full body makeover without the help of her parents.

The only problem she was facing was where she was going to get the money for this makeover.

Then all of a sudden she remembered what Virginia would say to her when she would come home after curfew. *"If you are going to lay up with a man, better make sure you get some money from him."* She remembered the times she spent with her aunt Tisha. Tisha was Mona's baby daughter who was certified in gold digging. It wasn't a man in her life who didn't pay for her time. Cinnamon would observe Tisha's interactions with numerous guys, and thought her aunt Tisha was the coolest person ever.

What caught Cinnamon's attention was the money, clothes , and jewelry her aunt Tisha received from being a certified hoe. She admired her, and actually looked up to her as a role model.

Cinnamon decided that the next guy who tried to get with her was going to pay for it.

One rainy morning on her way to school, ,a black guy in a white Cadillac pulled up to her while she stood at the bus stop pulled up in front of her and said, "Hi, beautiful, you need a ride?"

Cinnamon paid him no attention whatsoever, and politely looked in the opposite direction. "I got money," he said as he pulled out a stack of cash. She looked down the street and noticed that the bus was two stops away. She had to make a decision, and she had to make it quick, so she looked back at the guy and noticed that his smile was attractive. He had a gold tooth and waves in his hair that would make a person sea sick, LOL.

At that very moment, she decided to get in the car with him. She figured that she could use the money. *How else will I get that leather jacket with those Jordans,* she thought to herself as she quickly closed the car door.

"So, what's up, beautiful?" he seductively asked, as he licked his lips, but at the same time glancing over at Cinnamon's legs and thighs. He seemed to be a slightly tall, dark-skinned man who resembled Wesley Snipes. Unfortunately his breath was kicking like Jackie Chan, LOL. "How much are you talking about?" Cinnamon said before she realized she was talking off guard.

She had no idea how to negotiate a sex deal. "I need $200," she said directly. "Well, damn you ain't no Whitney Houston, little mama," he told her in a sweet slick kind of way. "Forget it then," Cinnamon said while reaching for the door attempting to get out of the car but calling his bluff at the same time.

"Okay, shorty, I can make that happen. Close my door, so we can take a ride," he told her.

He drove a few blocks down the street to this dead-end street. As soon as the car stopped, he didn't hesitate to pull his nasty ass little dick out. Cinnamon was only fifteen and was nervous as she entered the point of no return.

He opened up a lifestyle rubber and placed it on his Vienna sausage of a penis, LOL. He then looked at Cinnamon, instructed her to go to the backseat of the car and instructed her to remove her clothes. She did exactly what she was told. "Damn, you're beautiful, baby girl," were the words he whispered into her ear as he inserted himself inside of her. It was over before it began. *Damn, that's it?* Cinnamon thought to herself as he moaned and groaned in satisfaction.

He climbed off of her and handed her $200 plus a $50 tip because of how good it was. Cinnamon smiled as she felt a sense of power take over her body. She made $250 in less than five minutes. *I could do this all the time,* she thought to herself as she put her clothes back on and climbed her way to the front passenger seat.

The guy agreed to drop her off on Fordham Road where her school was located. Cinnamon happily decided to ditch school and go shopping. She purchased a new pair of Air Jordans, and a cute outfit to match

When she returned to her fathers house that evening, he noticed that she had on a new pair of sneakers. She hid her outfit inside of her back pack.

"Where did you get those sneakers from?" Her father asked with a serious look on his face that demanded the truth. Cinnamon immediately lied and told her father that her best friend let her borrow them. It seemed to work because he didn't say anything else about it.

As time went by Cinnamon continued to buy new sneakers and clothes, and her father continued to be nosy. It was becoming uncomfortable when her father and step mother would question her about where she is getting money from. Cinnamon decided to move back with Virginia at least she can do whatever she wanted without being questioned so much.

When Cinnamon would come home with bags of shoes and clothes Mona would be looking at Cinnamon with a disgusted look on her face. Even though she installed prostitution in Cinnamon's head, she really didn't think that she would actually go out and do it. Especially without breaking her off a few dollars, "so you ain't bring me shit ?" Virginia would question, "Let me get some mother fucking money; I know you don't think that you're going to live under my roof for free!!"

Cinnamon paid her ass no attention as she humbly walked to the bedroom.

The next day, Cinnamon decided to hang out with her girls. Cinnamon and her girls was so close that they called themselves 'GMC'. "The Get Money Chicks." Cinnamon, Jessica, Janae Stoney, Mo and 7/30 Kay were all part of the squad.

Every Friday was party time and the G.M.C girls looked forward to it. The girls would save up the little cash they got during the week so they could obtain a bottle of liquor and weed on Friday.

They were all under the age of eighteen, so they would pay a homeless drunk a dollar or two to purchase the bottle for them.

You can always find an alcoholic hanging out in front of mainly every liquor store in the Bronx. They got drunk and walked the streets, terrorizing people. They were careless and ruthless.

Cinnamon was loving life; she felt as though her friends were her real family. They respected and treated her way better than her original family, and she wouldn't trade them for the world. She finally obtained the image she had been chasing for so long—one which was keeping her hair, nails, eyebrows, and feet prim and proper. The other was buying the latest Jordans as soon as they came out. Everything seemed to be working out in her favor, and it was around this time that she found love.

She fell in love with a Harlem guy named Gordon. She met him through Jenae who was messing with his homeboy J. Every weekend, Janae and Cinnamon would go to Harlem faithfully. It was something about Harlem that amazed her. It was different from the Bronx. Harlem was lit to the maximum, and it was exciting to her.

Gordon was a handsome dark-skinned dude with a low haircut and big juicy lips. His lips were not the only thing that were juicy (if you know what I mean), his personality was amazing as well. He was like a comedian who could put a smile on anyone's face.

Janae and Cinnamon never smoked weed until they started going to Harlem. J and Gordon seemed to be very good at convincing the girls to try it. It wasn't long before Cinnamon started smoking weed regularly. She fell in love with the high instantly.

A few years went by, and Cinnamon was still fooling around with Gordon. She would show up at his house uninvited when she felt like it. Gordan would advise her to call before she came over, but he never seemed to pick up when she would call.

Cinnamon could feel deep down inside that she was not the only girl he was messing around with, but she didn't care just as long as she could be in his life.

There were times when Cinnamon went to Harlem, and Gordon would be entertaining other girls, and she would go home crying.

Within a few days, she would be right back in his arms. Janae couldn't understand why Cinnamon would allow Gordon to treat her that way. It was obvious to everyone that he didn't give a damn about her. Love starts within which means you can't love anyone or anything until you've mastered the love for self.

Reading the Holy Bible would be a great place to start the journey of self love.

Cinnamon pitifully looked at Janae and sincerely told her, "I love him." Unbeknownst to Janae, Cinnamon fell in love with Gordon the first day she laid eyes on him. All she wanted was for someone to love her unconditionally. Little did she know that she didn't have a clue about the true definition of love. Not only that, but Cinnamon didn't have a clue of what love looked like. She assumed that being reunited with her mother will fill that void that's been in her heart, but instead that hole in her heart has widened.

Unbeknownst to her, the love she craved was buried deep down within herself. She tolerated the disrespect all the way up until she decided to break it off with Gordan. He started fooling around with this Lisa Raye looking chic and that was the last straw for Cinnamon. Making that decision devastated her and she tried her hardest to embrace the pain.

Even though she was still having sex for money the whole time she was with Gordon, she loved him from head to toe.

After the break up with Gordon, she began smoking and drinking heavily. The streets were her comfort zone because she resented living with Virginia. To Cinnamon living there was like being in World War II because they bumped heads constantly.

Cinnamon spent most of her time at Jessica's house, and eventually ended up moving in. Jessica's mother Brenda didn't hesitate to open her door for Cinnamon.

It was something about Cinnamon that made Brenda want to be there for her. Brenda has been through some of the same things as Cinnamon, if not worse.

Brenda understood what it was to have a mother literally not give a damn about her child. Cinnamon made a promise to never do anything stronger than marijuana. She vowed to never neglect her future children. She vowed to love her kids unconditionally, and that no matter what, she would never be anything like her mother. She made a promise to herself, to not let her circumstances be the outcome of her future, and to make something out of her life.

CHAPTER 5

ON THE MOVE

Months after Cinnamon and Gordon's break up, Cinnamon felt as though she needed to get away. Two years ago, at the age of sixteen she pleaded with her mother to sign her up for the Job Corps. Job Corps is the largest Free residential education and job training program for young adults ages 16–24. Her mother's response to Cinnamon's request was to get the fuck out of her face. After years of begging her mother to sign her up, she decided to do it herself on her eighteenth birthday.

Job Corps was a place where teenagers could achieve the General Educational Development (GED),driver's license, and a trade. For some strange reason, it was like her mother did not want to see her progress. Her mother refused to support her by signing her up for a better future.

Cinnamon couldn't understand why her mother did not want her to do better with her life. It could have been because her life was Jack and cracked up. When Cinnamon turned eighteen, she did exactly what she said she would do, and signed herself up for the program.

Within two weeks her application was approved and she was on her way to a better future.

They placed her at Delaware Valley Job Corp. Center which was located at Callicoon, New York. When she arrived, she was ready to conquer the world and prove to everyone that she was gonna be somebody.

Cinnamon was ready to break the cycle and the statistics that said she was going to be a failure because of her upbringing … not on her watch.

They placed her in a room that had three twin size beds. It was two African American girls who were twin sisters that was responsible for giving Cinnamon a tour around the campus. Instead, they walked around looking for a Dutch. "I got one," said Cinnamon. "Roll that shit up," she said jokingly.

They instantly grew attached to each other. They were the kind of girls that Cinnamon could rock with. The next day was Intake , which meant that the students were required to take a physical and drug test.

Cinnamon failed the drug test and passed the physical.

Since she had just made it to Job Corps, they gave her thirty days to have her system cleaned. Smoking didn't affect her because in her mind, she was more focused on her goals and her purpose when marijuana was involved.

Cinnamon decided to study dental assistant, and she told herself that within six months she would have her Dental Assistant Trade and her GED. Six months have passed and she accomplished her goals. She's proven to herself that she could do whatever she put her mind to and as long as she put God first. After her internship, she found a part time job in Manhattan at a dental office on 42nd Street Grand Central.

Her friends were the only ones who cared that she did something with herself. Mona, Virginia and Cinnamon's dad could care less. She shook off the negative energy and remained focused on her life and goals.

She was eighteen years old, and she was a dental assistant which made her feel really good about herself.

She finally was happy and content with her life.

Everything was going good until she reached out to Gordon. She was missing him so much that she decided to stop by his house one day. They talked for a while, and he informed her that he was still fooling around with that chic who looked like Lisa Raye.

Cinnamon and Gordon hung out the whole night, drinking and reminiscing about the fun times they used to have when they were together. He told her how much he missed her and how crazy his new girlfriend was. He made sweet love to her and just like that, once again, he was hooked and so was she.

Gordon's sex was the best sex she ever had. It was as if their spirits slowly danced with one another. It was magical; he knew all the right spots to hit at the right times.

Cinnamon continued to work and definitely party hard like a rock star.

The GMC crew members met up every Friday at Janae's house where they would drink, smoke lots of weed and have the greatest times of their lives.

There was a lot of action going on at Janae's mothers house from cookouts, fights, to the wildest parties.

The closest out of the clique was Cinnamon and Jessica; they did everything together. If you saw one, you were going to see the other. They were inseparable and beneficial to one another.

Everything Cinnamon lacked, Jessica excelled and vice-versa. Jessica was the type of person who was a massive manipulator. By having a conversation with someone, she was able to tell their weaknesses. She could convince a person to do whatever she wanted.

Cinnamon was a little jealous of how she was able to adapt so easily around people. For as long as Cinnamon could remember, she has yearned to be accepted and loved by other people. That will be a fantasy she craved to turn into reality, and a fantasy that will lead her to self destruction.

One of the things that Jessica and Cinnamon bonded over was the terrible relationship with their mother. Cinnamon was getting kicked out of the house every other day. She spent the majority of her time at Jessica's house and decided to move in for a while.

Jessica's mom Brenda treated Cinnamon better than she did Jessica only because when she looked into Cinnamon 's eyes, she saw herself. They encounter the same sexual and physical abuse by the hands of someone they once trusted.. Brenda hated the way Cinnamon was being treated by her mother, and her door was always open for Cinnamon, no matter what the situation was.

A little time passed, and Cinnamon and Jessica's friendship was stronger than before. To be completely honest, Jessica was the only one she trusted. She would have given her life for Jessica if needed, and vice versa, or so she thought.

It was the summer of 2004, and everybody knows that NYC is full of excitement during the summer. Cinnamon and her girls were hanging out on the block, chilling at the neighborhood park. There were numerous other people who were hanging out as well. Cinnamon got into an altercation with this loud mouthed chick who thought she was a gangster. She actually thought she was going to talk to Cinnamon in a disrespectful tone. Cinnamon straight punched her in her mouth, and it was on from there. They fought like boxers in a ring. Cinnamon had blood all over her shirt, and it wasn't her blood.

The chic couldn't see her. Cinnamon's hands were like Muhammad Ali. They fought for about fifteen minutes until the point of exhaustion. All Cinnamon could hear was the girl's cousin telling her to keep on fighting.``Punch that bitch in her face" is what her cousin was screaming.

Cinnamon had no more fight in her, so she called out for Jessica to fight or at least punch the loud mouth cousin in her big as mouth.

"Yooo Jessica, Jessica…" Cinnamon shouted , but Jessica was nowhere in sight.

Janae noticed Jessica running in the direction of her house. Janae grabbed Cinnamon by her arm and told her "let just get the hell out of here,I got you don't worry,"

"I know, but where's Jessica? I need her here with me," cried Cinnamon.

Next thing she knew, the chick Cinnamon was fighting came out of nowhere and punched Cinnamon on the right side of her face. She instantly hit the floor. Her opponent along with two other girls started kicking her. Janae was furious so she ran up on one of the girls and brutally smacked one upside her head with a glass bottle.

Janae was quiet; she was the pacemaker out of the crew, always smiling and peaceful, but on that day Janae turnt into a beast. The other girls from the GMC crew ran like some little cowards. The last person Cinnamon expected to help her fight was Janae. She had more heart than the rest of them, and her loyalty was proven on that day.

After the fight, Cinnamon was exhausted and left the scene. She was so furious at the fact that Jessica got scared and ran. It was hard for her to understand it because she would have never done that to her; if anything, Cinnamon would have taken that as whooping with her.

Rule number one was to never leave each other hanging EVER!!

Jessica broke that rule, and she would pay for that decision. It will be a long time before Cinnamon even thought about forgiving Jessica. To be honest things will never be the same between the two. She looked at Jessica as if she was a phony and fake; she felt as though she didn't know who the hell Jessica was, and she didn't trust her anymore.

Cinnamon was crying out for Jessica, and Jessica left her for dead. She felt like Jessica was a coward and a traitor. Cinnamon rested for a while at her mom's house for an hour or so before she headed to Jessica's house. She wanted an explanation on why she left her hanging; it was either that or they were going to fight.

Cinnamon knocked on Jessica's mom's door, and there was no answer. She knew exactly where she was. She was next door at her god brother's house. Cinnamon furiously banged on the god brothers door until he answered. Once the door was opened she rushed past him without saying hello and headed straight to where Jessica was sitting. "Yo, WTF happened?" yelled Cinnamon with rage written all over her face. Jessica explained that she thought everybody was going home, so she went home. Cinnamon knew it was bullshit because someone said they saw Jessica running up the street when the girl's cousin started instigating the fight. Cinnamon knew the street code which was: if your home boy or home girl run from a fight, then they deserve to get their ass whooped. PERIOD!

Cinnamon had so much love for Jessica and decided to not put hands on her. Instead she let karma have its way with little miss Jessica and emotionally gravitated herself away from their friendship.

As time went on GMC remained close, but that fight definitely put a strain on their friendship. Cinnamon continued working in the medical field and continued her relationship with Gordon.

Her bad choices in life finally caught up with her when she found out that she was pregnant. What made it worse was that she had no idea who the father could be.

CHAPTER 6

TAKING THE GOOD
WITH THE BAD

Cinnamon was nineteen years old and pregnant with no stable place to live. She was still working as a dental assistant but that was only part-time. The first trimester for her was pure hell; She was so sick that she couldn't get out of bed. Everything she ate, she was throwing up .

It was a horrible experience for her and things only took a turn for the worst when she broke the news to Gordon.

He didn't seem too happy about it, one reason being because some girl from his neighbor was claiming to be pregnant by him as well. To make matters worse Cinnamon and the girl was due two months apart.

Virginia made it loud and clear that Cinnamon was not bringing any babies into her house. Cinnamon didn't have anywhere to live. At seven months pregnant, her only option was to enter into a temporary homeless shelter located in Manhattan.

A month after being in the shelter, she was placed in a long term shelter in Poughkeepsie, New York.

A week after arriving in Poughkeepsie, she received news that Jessica was pregnant. Cinnamon was having a baby boy in August, and Jessica was expecting a baby girl in January. It was odd because Cinnamon always wanted a daughter and Jessica always dreamed of having a son. I guess, in life, you can't always have what you want.

The shelter was actually a 9 bedroom house with a huge dining room and kitchen. The backyard was humongous with a slide and swing set up to occupy the children residing there.

Poughkeepsie opened her eyes to the importance of faith and religion. She knew that it was God who brought her to Poughkeepsie. It will be her God who she depended on to lead her through this chapter of her life. The lord blessed her with the roof over her head, clothing as well as a hot meal everyday. Trust and believe that she was more than thankful and filled with grace.

In the rear section of the dining room was a mini church.On Sundays, a preacher would come to the house to preach the Word of God to whoever was interested.

Every so often during the late night hours when everyone was asleep,Cinnamon would go to the altar to cry and pray for better days.

Being pregnant in the hot humid summer was overwhelming and with a month and three weeks left to go Cinnamon couldn't wait. Cinnamon woke up filled with excitement as she got herself together for her doctor's appointment. She spent hours waiting for the results of her glucose test. When the doctor finally read her the results , she instantly became speechless. The results revealed that she had Gestational diabetes which is a form

of diabetes while pregnant. One of the effects was that her baby will continue to rapidly gain weight. Her doctor decided that she would have to have an emergency C-section.

At that time she was eight months pregnant, and the baby was close to nine pounds. Doctor informed her that if he didn't perform an emergency C-section, her baby's weight would reach up to twelve pounds within the next month. It was the scariest moment of her life and she dreaded being alone.She decided to inform Gordan and Jessica about the situation and neither one of them hesitated to be by her side..Jessica, Gordon, and Gordon's mother showed their support by coming to the hospital for the birth of the baby. Her son was a beautiful eight-pound baby boy whom she named Michael.

Cinnamon was ecstatic,and filled with joy as she held him in her arms. Upon leaving the hospital and making it back to the shelter with her little angel Cinnamon was confused because she was filled with undesirable emotions. She was amazed at how Micheal stayed asleep the whole night. It scared the hell out of Cinnamon because most newborns woke up at least three or four times in a single night. She had to make sure he was okay by waking him up to feed him. Being a mother was the best thing that happened to her.

The social workers who ran the shelter informed all residents that they would not assist with financing permanent residence. In other words if the residents were seeking permanent housing they were one their own. The following month, Jessica convinced Cinnamon to move in with her and her mother. She was always welcome with open arms and knew for a fact that her son will be welcome as well.

When she got there, Brenda was very sick, and she wasn't able to move around. She had numerous heart surgeries and had cancer as well. The doctor gave her six months to live; unfortunately, she didn't live long enough to see Jessica give birth to her only granddaughter. She would often tell Cinnamon and Jessica to stick together because they were all they had.

Jessica listened, but Cinnamon was stubborn and hardheaded and didn't pay her heed. She didn't trust Jessica anymore and lost a lot of love for her after what happened that day when she left Cinnamon for dead.When Brenda passed away, their friendship became estranged and Jessica was mad that Cinnamon didn't attend the funeral.

Her reason for not going to the funeral was because she didn't want to see Brenda laying in her casket and didn't want to remember her that way. It would have been unbearable for her to handle. Instead, she wanted to remember Brenda as being the strong black woman that she was.

Jessica didn't understand it and felt as though Cinnamon was being selfish. They got into a big fight after Brenda passed away, and Cinnamon decided to leave Brenda's apartment to go into a shelter yet again.

Cinnamon was in the shelter for three months and was so close to getting her apartment, but ended up getting kicked out because she violated her curfew. It seemed as though things couldn't go right for her.

Cinnamon had to start over again and this made her furious. She ended up getting rejected from every shelter that she applied for, so she made the decision to move down south to Mississippi.

Ironically Virginia was moving down there as well only because the city was going to use her building into a homeless shelter.

Besides that Mona practically begged Cinnamon to relocate to Mississippi. She was anxious to meet her great grandson.

Cinnamon's mind was made up, she was leaving New York City for good, and two weeks later she and Michael were on the Greyhound Bus headed south. Cinnamon and her son reached Mississippi a day and a half later at exactly 3:45 a.m. When she arrived, her grandmother Mona was waiting there for her.

Mona was there waiting for her Cinnamon along with her neighbor and her neighbor's husband who drove thirty minutes to the bus station. When Cinnamon got into the car, she noticed that something was off about the married couple, but Cinnamon couldn't put her finger on it. It was like they were trying really hard to impress her by degrading one another.

By the time she made it to Mona's house, she was exhausted and decided to take her and the baby a hot bath. Afterwards, she laid her baby down in her old bed. She lied down beside him and started to put together a plan. She decided to go to a four-year college to get a degree in nursing. Afterwards she would move back to New York where she could make some real money. Unfortunately sometimes things don't always turn out the way we would like them to.

The weird couple had a son that was living with them named Nate. He wasn't attractive. He had a long face with braids, stood about five-feet eleven inches tall and weighed 140 pounds. Every time he smiled, all you could see was gums. Cinnamon remembered him from junior high school. He was always wild and crazy. Back then Nate had the biggest crush on Cinnamon from the first time he saw her.

It wasn't a surprise that he wanted her when he found out that she was back in Mississippi. Every day for a whole two weeks, he would shower her with gifts, not only for her, but for her son as well. That right there was a bonus in Cinnamon's eyes, she loved being spoiled.

She really didn't want to get into a serious relationship because of what she had gone through with Gordon, besides, a relationship was the last thing on her mind.

She ended up giving Nate a chance which turned out to be a decision that would change her life forever. Nate's family was the one of the worst people on the planet, people would warn her about the family, but she would brush it off because she wasn't one who listened to gossip.

What was crazy was that his family didn't like Cinnamon from day one, most likely jealousy was the motive. He had three messy, grimy sisters and his no teeth having ass mother was the ringleader.

They interfered in his matters for two reasons – the first one is because he told them every fucking thing, and second one is because they had no life of their own. He had a daughter the same age as Cinnamon's son by this woman he said he was using for money.

"Dick went in and money came out," is the way he described the relationship to Cinnamon. She was not attractive at all and Nate was embarrassed to tell anyone that he had a baby with her.

When he found out she was pregnant, he denied the baby all the way up until a paternity test was done. Even then, he still didn't want anything to do with his daughter.

The only time he got to see the baby was when his mother would go out of her way, drive to her house and pick her up from

Her mother's house for holidays , and sometimes weekends.

One rainy afternoon, Cinnamon's grandmother Mona pulled her to the side to talk to her. She told Cinnamon about how Nate would physically abuse his child's mother, not only that, but a week before Cinnamon got to Mississippi, The three of Nate's sisters jumped the girl Nate had his daughter with.

Instantly, she put her guard up and made her mind up that she was not gonna mess with Nate's family including his mother whom Cinnamon nicknamed "mother dearest".

Besides all of the drama, Cinnamon found herself falling in love with Nate. She fell head over heels for Nate. He said all the right things at the right time. They had fun together. Every Friday, they went out to the club and party like rock stars. She was in love, and Nate treated her like a queen or so she thought.

Cinnamon thought that no other chic wanted him because of his looks. Boy, was she wrong! Things started to get a little crazy with his family when

Nate's sister would tell him all these crazy things about Cinnamon, and he believed every lie she told, such as her cheating and fooling with other guys. Nate's mother's house was right next-door to Mona's. house.

Cinnamon couldn't take the drama any longer so she gave Nate an ultimatum that if he didn't get them a place of their own, she was leaving him……PERIOD!. Nate got his taxes the next month and moved them into a three-bedroom trailer. A couple of weeks prior he lost his job detailing cars, might have been so he could keep an eye on Cinnamon. The both of them applied for a position at a chicken plant. Cinnamon was hired and Nate wasn't. The both of them decided on Nate staying home with Michael, or so she thought. When she would fo

to work, Nate would drop Michael off with Miss Mona while he ran the streets.

They were only six months into the relationship when he brought a woman into their bed to have sex while Cinnamon was working. Come to find out the girl he cheated with was his sister's best friend. Cinnamon vowed to never let a man treat her the way Gordon did. Cinnamon packed up a few things and left his ass in that trailer looking pitiful. She stayed gone for about two weeks before she went back home and forgave him for cheating on her.

The whole time she was gone he showered her with gifts. He cried, begged, and promised to never do it again. He convinced Cinnamon that she was the love of his life and that he wanted to marry her. She was convinced that he would go above and beyond to keep her in his life. She believed him, and a few months later, he cheated again. Cinnamon found herself in a deep depression; his mother and sisters were still actively involved in their relationship.Nate had a knack of telling his mom every little detail of their relationship. Nate gave Cinnamon something that she has been yearning for ever since she was a little girl.

She never had unconditional love. Nobody showed Cinnamon any type of affection and love. Nate cared when Cinnamon left his sight. He actually cried for her to come back to him. Cinnamon figured that this must really be love, and he loved her more than life itself. If this was not love, then what is it? Wasthe thoughts that ran through her head. She was young and naïve,and Nate took advantage of her cravings for real love. Love was something that Cinnamon craved.

If loving him was wrong she did not want to be right; it started to get real when she found out she was pregnant in 2008. That's when the heat between Cinnamon, mother dearest, and the sisters started to fire up. They pretended to be happy to have Cinnamon as a new family member. She didn't have to buy a thing for the baby because Nate's mother bought everything.

It was like she was trying to buy Cinnamon's respect. Cinnamon thought it was pathetic for a grown woman to desperately buy someone friendship. Summer of 2009, she gave birth to the most beautiful baby boy ever. He was her heart and joy. It was the beginning of the hell that was to come; it was the end of her serenity. What she was about to experience would change her life for the better and for the worse.

CHAPTER 7

HELL'S KITCHEN

There was something about drugs and addiction that terrified Cinnamon. Every time she would think about the consequences of addiction, she vowed to stay away from it. Her worst fear was becoming an addict as well as repeating the same toxic cycle as her mother.

Her mother lost custody of her children because of her addiction, unfortunately the drugs controlled her every move. Cinnamon would rather have died than become like her mom. Life has a funny way of teaching you that you should never say never. Even though hard drugs scared her, it didn't stop her from smoking weed on an everyday basis since the age of sixteen, and it didn't take long for her to fall in love with it.

Cinnamon was twenty years old at the time when she tried cocaine and she fell in love with it.

All of this took place prior to moving to Mississippi. The cocaine in Mississippi was not as good as the Cocaine in New York.

She stopped using it for a while and it wasn't until she had her second son that she fell into this deep depression and started using cocaine yet again.

Not only did she start using, she introduced Nate to the highly addictive drug. It started off as a recreational thing—something they did on the weekends. Then they gradually moved up the ladder and made it a everyday thing. They were like Bobby and Whitney, and Bonnie and Clyde. When you saw one, you saw the other; they were inseparable. It seemed like the cocaine made them a little closer.

Their consumption became so much that they had threesomes sex parties and indulged in all types of different sexual acts. She would go out and hit licks which meant she would seduce different guys to pay to play with the approval of Nate of course. Cinnamon would come back with a few hundred dollars, only to spend it on alcohol and drugs.

Cinnamon always had this thing for drug dealers only because they spent money just as fast as they got it. Her uncle Roy introduced her to this low-key hustler named Mack. Even though her uncle Roy molested her when she was a little girl Cinnamon was trained to sweep her emotions under the rug which is why she hasn't told anyone about the incident. Her uncle Roy's reason for introducing Cinnamon to Mack is because he was hoping Mack would be nice enough to give him drugs for the introduction. Cinnamon was young and gorgeous, her uncle Roy knew Mack would be attracted to her; in other words, her uncle pimped her out to get high.

Mack wasn't that attractive, but he had what Cinnamon loved— money. Mack was kind of a cornball in Cinnamon's eyes, but he showed how much he wanted her by showering her with gifts as well as everything she asked him for.

Mack stood about five-feet eleven-inches tall, weighing a mere 260 pounds. He had a chocolate-colored complexion along with a full beard and mustache. What made him stand out from any other man was his high-pitch voice that sounded like a woman. He had a voice like Mike Tyson.

If you were to talk to him on the phone without knowing him, you would assume he was a woman. One night, Mack and Cinnamon snuck away together. As they were chilling and drinking, Cinnamon got an urge to get high. Mack told her that he was out of cocaine. She knew he was lying; she could feel it.

Then, out of nowhere, Mack told her he has something else and asks if she wants it. She looked over at him and noticed that he had the biggest and ugliest smile on his face. Little did she know, Mack has been planning on getting her hooked on crack for the longest. Mack figured if he could turn Cinnamon into a certified junkie she would be under his control. He would lie and tell her that he ran out of cocaine when in fact he was loaded with cocaine. The lies went on for a while, and every time Cinnamon would reject Mack when he offered her crack.

One thing everyone knows about Mack is that he never runs out of crack. He was so in love with her that he hated the fact that she was in love with Nate. Mack resented Nate, and wanted Cinnamon all to himself. He wanted her mind, body, and soul. One Friday night after a brutal beating from Nate Cinnamon was vulnerable and at a breaking point, and decided to hook up with Mack. She asked him for some cocaine, and yet again he said he didn't have any, and offered her crack instead.

"Whatever, I don't care; just let me get it," said Cinnamon, instantly grabbing the four pieces of crack rocks he laid on the table. She smashed it up and began to snort it up her nose. The effect was not the same as cocaine, so she decided to roll it up in rolling papers along with tobacco. From then on, every time they met, it was crack-cocaine mixed with tobacco, liquor, and marijuana.

The feeling that she felt when she smoked the crack with tobacco made her want more and more. It took months before her and Mack interacted sexually. Being high as a kite was the only reason Cinnamon decided to give Mack some pussy.

All the while Nate had no idea about what she and Mack had going on. Nate was too busy chasing women, as long as Cinnamon brought back drugs and money he was happy.

Cinnamon thought that she was getting over on Mack, but it was the other way around. Mack was destroying her only because she would not choose him over Nate.

Mack had a plan for her which was to have her hooked, so hook that eventually she'll become a junkie. Once Cinnamon was hooked on crack, she would be on her knees begging to be with him.

Nate could sense that Cinnamon was being unfaithful, but he couldn't prove it. When people in town would come back and tell Nate that they saw Cinnamon and Mack together, that was all the confirmation that Nate needed.

He became so angry about the situation that he binged off of cocaine for forty-eight hours. When he finally made it home from partying he beat the hell out of Cinnamon for hours. After the beating, he wrapped his hands around her neck and squeezed it as hard as he could.

Cinnamon eyes begin to roll in the back of her head, and she could feel herself drifting in and out of consciousness.

Even though it lasted two minutes, it felt like eternity. Her eyes then begin to feel as if they were about to pop out of her socket, and that's when Nate let her go. If he had held her a minute longer, she would have been dead. Nate was losing it, the drugs were taken over his mind, and Cinnamon could feel death getting closer and closer by the second.

There was no doubt in her mind that she had to get away from Nate, but she was too afraid. There was no one around that had the balls to stand up against Nate and his family, nobody DARED!!

Mother dearest (Nates mother) was a tall slim lady who was about five-feet eleven-inches and weighed about 139 pounds. She would talk so loudly, you could hear her before you saw her. She loved attention; it didn't matter if it was good attention or bad attention as long as she got it. She lost her temper within a blink of an eye if she felt disrespected.

It was obvious that mother dearest was mentally unstable. The town that they lived in was a very small town in Mississippi where everybody knew everybody.

One day while sitting outside, Mona sat beside Cinnamon and they started to converse about mother dearest. Mona told Cinnamon about one of their relatives who was cool with mother dearest. Cinnamon's relative and mother dearest got into a heated argument. Mother dearest walked up to Cinnamon's relative with a blade in her hand and slid it across the face of Cinnamon's relative, then walked away like it was nothing.

The thing was that mother dearest had strings she could pull. She knew people that knew people who could get her out of trouble. There was one person that mother dearest couldn't stand—CINNAMON.

She felt as though Cinnamon turnt her son into the junkie that he was. She vowed to do to Cinnamon what she had done to her, destroy the only thing she cared about most….. HER CHILDREN.

From then on, mother dearest secretly declared war on Cinnamon. The first step was to hook Nate up with as many women as possible. She hooked him up with one of theses twins who were supposed to be staying with her because they were homeless. He ended up messing around with both of them, the were younger than eighteen.

She had another plan: to take full custody of Cinnamon's children. Mother dearest was waiting for the perfect moment for Cinnamon to slip up. Unbeknownst to Cinnamons that moment would come sooner than she thought. Cinnamon messed up and she messed up badly. Mother dearest was ready to put her evil plan into action.

One night after partying, Cinnamon and Nate got into a real nasty fight over the one and only "Mack." He threatened to kill her if she didn't tell him the truth about her relationship with Mack. Terrified, Cinnamon told him everything from the beginning until the end. Afterwards Nate sent her to hit a lick with Mack. Which meant that she was to do whatever it took to bring that money back to Nate.

Hours passed when Nate realized that Cinnamon was taking way too long to come back, and besides that, she wasn't answering her phone.

When she finally decided to come home, she was empty-handed or at least that's what she wanted Nate to believe. He punched her in her mouth, before beating the shit out of her and dislocating her nose. It started that Saturday night and it didn't end until Sunday afternoon.

She looked out of the window and noticed Nate's sister standing not too far from the house listening and being nosy. Cinnamon figured that if she got his sister's attention maybe that would help her escape Nate's abuse or at least calm him down. She banged on the window yelling for them to call the police.

Cinnamon had to have been losing her mind if she thought they really gave a damn about her getting her ass beat. Either that or she was still high to even think that any one of Nate's family would come to her rescue. They might have been the ones to encourage the ass whooping she was getting from him.

Mother dearest had all of her children under her evil spell. In fact, she was the one who decided to call the police. Once Nate heard one of the sister scream, "The cops are on their way," he grabbed the keys to the truck and yelled at Cinnamon to get the fuck in the truck.

When his sister watched her hop inside the truck alongside with Nate after getting her ass beat, they yelled out, "You dumb bitch, you're going to leave with that nigga." Nate and Cinnamon sped off as if they just committed murder. Nate calmly informed Cinnamon that they would return when things died down, but little did they know that shit was about to get turned the hell up.

Their living situation was complicated so let me give you the run-down. Okay during the entire 4 years of Cinnamon and Nate's relationship she has left him over six times. She would wait until Nate left the house only because he would do anything and everything to stop her even murder. When a woman is in an abusive relationship, the number one rule is never let your abuser know when you are about to leave because it can cost you your life.

By the time Nate would make it back home Cinnamon and the kids would be gone.

This particular time Cinnamon relocated to Atlanta where Jessica was living with her baby and her boyfriend.

Jessica's baby's father was from Atlanta, so Jessica moved down there to be with him after her daughter was born. Jessica and Cinnamon never lost contact with one another, and were still in each other's life. During the particular breakup, Cinnamon relocated to Atlanta with Jessica and her baby's father. At that time Jessica has been with him for a couple of years. Living in Atlanta didn't stop Cinnamon from doing what she knew how to do best. She tricked men out of their money for drugs and whatever else she wanted. The stress from her relationship with Nate only increased the urge to escape reality. There wasn't a day that went by that she wasn't high or smiling in a dude face to get high.. Jessica and her baby father were having problems in their relationship that resulted in Jessica sleeping on the living couch instead of her bedroom. One night after getting wasted and I mean wasted off of every drug you can think of, Cinnamon obliviously opened the door to Jessica's bedroom. It had to be around 4 a.m while everyone in the house was asleep. In a drunken daze, Cinnamon stood at the door, and blew a kiss at Jessica's baby father as he laid down in his bed watching a movie.

She seductively placed both hands on her nipples and proceeded to rub in a circular motion while licking her lips. Jessica's baby father was confused and figured Jessica used Cinnamon to see how faithful and loyal he really was. That's when he aggressively told Cinnamon to get the hell out of his room. Not only that but he told her that she better tell Jessica that she tried to fuck him or else he would.

Cinnamon instantly snapped back to reality after feeling like she was sleep walking. Realizing what had just taken place, she was instantly filled with undesirable emotions. She slowly closed his bedroom door, and shamefully walked away. She laid down on her bed staring at the ceiling thinking about what the hell she was going to do. Not too long ago she received her federal taxes on her debit card, so money wasn't an issue. The drugs took over and turned her into somebody she didn't recognize. Trying to sleep with your best friend's boyfriend was the ultimate betrayal, more less unforgivable .Before she could explain what happened Jessica's baby father beat her to the punch, and told her everything. The look on Jessica's face looked like a bow and arrow had pierced through her heart, and what he was telling her could not be true.She slowly turned around to look Cinnamon in her eyes, in doing so this told her everything she needed to know. The realization of her best friend's betrayal hit her like a bomb and resulted in her storming out of the house. That was the last time Cinnamon would see or hear from Jessica. Cinnamon felt like a piece of shit and told herself the reason why her mother hated her was because she was the worst person on the planet. Not once did she think about the repercussions of her actions. *What was she thinking?Was she really going to fuck Jessica's man then smile in her face afterwards?* A blind man could see that the drugs had taken over, and Cinnamon was no longer in control of her actions. Cinnamon and Jessica's friendship was finally over, and it will never be the same. The next day Cinnamon and her two boys headed back to Mississippi, back to Nate. By the time Cinnamon made it back to Mississippi she realized that she left her debit card on Jessica's kitchen counter. She quickly made a phone call to have her card canceled, they advised her that she would receive another card in two weeks. At that time Mona left Mississippi and relocated to New York. Her house was vacant and it definitely wasn't livable. The paint on the walls was chipping, the ceiling would leak every time it rained, in other words it was horrible, and unlivable.

Cinnamon's plan was to stay at Mona's abandon house until she received her new debit card in the mail. Once she received her card she planned on finding a stable place of her own far away from Nate's family. Im

Not sure if I told you guys that Mona's house was located directly beside Nate's mother's house. Which was the reason Cinnamon let her boys sleep over there every night, while she and Nate slept at Mona's. Mona's house was in no condition for anyone to be staying there, definitely not any children.

Let me remind you that after all the fighting Nate and Cinnamon have been doing, the house was five times worse than it actually was. Walking inside the house you would have thought that a hurricane had passed through it. Okay, so that was the rundown of Cinnamon and Nate were sitting in the truck not too far from the house when the police pulled into Mother dearest yard. When the police arrived, mother dearest approached the cops before they could get out of their vehicle. "Hey officer, how are you?" she asked. Before he could answer she blurted out "my son and his girlfriend are on drugs,and all they do is fight all day, every day, around their kids". Looking pitiful she continued on by saying, they are stealing and prostituting for drugs, and the house they live in is unsuitable for these children" she said as she slowly started walking in the direction of Mona's house. She turned around to see if the officers were behind her. "Come take a look at the type of environment they have their children living in," she continued. The officer looked at her and said, "Ma'am, we are not allowed to walk inside of the home without permission from the owner."

Mother dearest looked the officer dead in his eyes and said, "Sir, do you think I would ask you to come inside a house that is not mine?" The officer didn't argue with her as he followed her into the house. "See what I mean," mother dearest said as she pointed at the shattered glass that was on the floor from a broken window in the bedroom. "This doesn't make no damn sense, someone needs to get the Department of human services involved", said mother dearest.

The officer looked at the expression on her face and noticed her eyes becoming watery. Mother dearest thought about the miscarriages she'd had, so she could be sad enough to cry.

Whatever she did worked because the police officer nodded his head up and down in agreement before walking to his car to make a call. Mother dearest was on his trail listening to every single word that came out of the officer's mouth.

"Ma'am I have just notified the supervisor of the Department of Human Services. She concluded that you along with the parents are scheduled to attend a meeting with the social workers at 9:00 a.m Monday morning at the Department of Human Services. I must inform you that the Supervisor recommended that kids stay with you until further notice . Do not, I repeat, do not let the kids leave with their parents. If you have any problems with the children's parents, please call me personally. Here's my card."the officer informed her right before cranking up his vehicle.

"Yes, sir, thank you," mother dearest said as the officer slowly bagged out of her yard and drove off. Mother dearest felt as if she could do backflips. She was over excited that her scheme had actually worked. She finally got the upper hand on Cinnamon, snd she was ecstatic. It was her only chance to pay Cinnamon back for turning her first born into an addict.

Cinnamon and Nate pulled up into his mother's yard twenty minutes after the police officers left.

Cinnamon and Nate sat in the truck quietly for a couple of minutes, until Nate decided to walk over to his mother's house to see what the hell was going on, and told Cinnamon to stay her motherfucking ass to stayin the car.

Ten minutes later Cinnamon was startled by a loud noise. It was Nate storming out of his mother's house in a rage as he slammed the front door yelling."Mother fuck that stupid bitch!!".

He opened the driver seat door and aggressively sat down.

Cinnamon looked at him before curiously asking "who are you talking about Nate?". Before speaking he puts his head down, punches the steering wheel then aggressively informs Cinnamon that his mother told the police a bunch of bullshit. The police officer called The Department of Human Services. That phone call resulted in the two of them having to go down to The Department of Human Services tomorrow morning to discuss the well-being of their children. In the meantime the kids are to stay with his mother until further notice.

Cinnamon couldn't believe her ears, she had to pinch herself to see if she was dreaming. It really didn't hit her until the next day when she met with the social workers at the department of human services. Cinnamon and Nate was the last ones to come in for the meeting.

As soon as they walked in the door everyone got quiet. It was obvious who they were talking about because they wer looking stupid as Nate and Cinnamon sat down in two empty seat at the rear end of the table.It was like a fucking board meeting of "Let's all team up on Cinnamon day." Before the meeting began the supervisor asked everyone to introduce themselves, and their relationship to the children. Afterwards they proceeded with the meeting starting with mother dearest. It was two caseworkers and a supervisor who sat beside one another at a long wooden desk. Linda the supervisor had a look on her face that read "Child, how the hell did you get caught up in this messy heartless ass family?"

Then there was a social worker on the left of Linda, whose name was Tina. She had a smile that could light up a room, but when you look in her eyes, it was like looking at the devil himself. Tina was a heavyset dark-skinned woman who couldn't bear any children. She held this underline hatred for women who could. If she couldn't have kids she didn't want anyone else to have theirs. What made matters worse was her husband of 8 years pressured her on a daily basis for a son.

On the right of Linda was a social worker named Julia. Julia was slightly tall, with long natural hair, dark beautiful complexion and petite.What made her stand out was her thick black glasses that were bigger than her face. She sat there nodding her head up and down in agreement with every word that came out of Tina's mouth.

Out of all the stuff that was coming out of Tina's mouth, she said something that Cinnamon will never forget. "You leave us no choice but to place the boys under the care of mother dearest for three months. Let me ask you guys a question." Tina looked at Nate and Cinnamon in their eyes and asked, "if I was to give you both a drug test, would you pass it?" Nate and Cinnamon looked at each other.

Tina pulled out a drug test and placed them on the table. That's when Cinnamon looked over at mother dearest who was enjoying every second of the interrogation. Cinnamon wanted to reach across the table and ring her fucking throat, but decided it wasn't a place or time to catch a murder case. Tina could feel the tension in the room and decided to ask again. "So, like I said, if I was to give you a drug test, would you pass?" Cinnamon turnt to her left where Nate was and could tell that he was about to explode.. "This is some mother-fucking bullshit," he angrily shouted, as he stormed out of the office.

In doing so, he scared the hell out of Tina's fat ass.

He scared her even more when he came back again and slammed the door four more times in a row "boom…boom…boom…boom." That's when Cinnamon got up and threw her chair towards mother 's dearest head. Lucky for her, she ducked, and the chair hit the wall instead.

Cinnamon paused for a minute before she ran out after her man. When she got outside, Nate was sitting down smoking a cigarette. "Let me hit that shit," she said while approaching him. "We will be alright, babe. We just have to do what we have to do to make it right. He stood up and the both of them calmly walked back into the office.

Cinnamon walked into the office with Nate right behind her. She looked Tina in her eyes and said, "There's no way that we can pass a drug test today or tomorrow either." Tina then asked her if she had any relatives that would take her two boys, who were ages three and six.

Before anyone could say anything, mother dearest had to add her two cents by saying,

"No, they are on crack and her mother is sick." Cinnamon said nothing because she knew she was right. If Cinnamon would've denied it, Tina would have asked her Virginia to take a drug test.

One thing was for sure and two things were certain. She didn't want her boys to be separated or be sent to a foster home.

She was backed up in a corner; she had no other relatives that would take her boys.

Tina then asked her if she would rather her kids be placed with an unknown family or with mother dearest. Cinnamon thought long and hard, not only for her boys, but for herself as well. She couldn't believe what she was about to say. " I'd rather have them stay with mother dearest" she nervously stated. Those words left a bitter taste in her mouth. Tina placed some papers in front of both Cinnamon and Nate. "Well, in this agreement, it is stated that you have three months to find suitable housing, a job, and attend Narcotic Anonymous meetings.

You also have visitation with the kids on Mondays and Thursdays at 3:30 p.m. here at this location. In three months from now, we'll take this matter to the judge, and then, go from there. I need you guys to date and sign here please." They grabbed the pen, and signed all of the forms that were placed in front of them. Afterwards Cinnamon started to feel dizzy and light-headed.

If it wasn't for the chair and table that was behind her, she would have hit the floor.

Everything became so clear to Cinnamon, she was walking the same path as her mother Virginia.

The woman that she vowed to never be like, not only that, but mother dearest had complete control over Cinnamon and her children.

Her life was in mother dearest's hands only because her children were her life. Without them, there was no point in living; she would rather be dead than live without her boys.

Nate and Cinnamon were feeling good about the situation. They… well, let's rephrase that. Cinnamon obtained a three-bedroom trailer and found N/A meetings to attend. She attended meetings as much as possible; she even walked in the rain to attend meetings.

Nate lingered along to a few meetings, but it seemed as though Nate could care less about making meetings and getting clean. At the end of the day, their two boys were with his mother which meant that he didn't have to put in as much effort as Cinnamon.

They were still getting high as a kite almost every other day. Ironically, Cinnamon had no idea that Nate was hired as an informant by mother dearest to keep a tab on Cinnamon.

Every move Cinnamon made, as far as getting high and turning tricks to pay for drugs was concerned, was reported by Nate. He would have a full report on who she fucked, and how much she got. He was a low-key dirty trader, and everyone could see it, except Cinnamon. He had her fooled and this caused her to have major depression. In fact, it wasn't until she moved to Mississippi when was diagnosed with anxiety and depression. Sadly mother dearest and Nate took advantage of that along with taking away her kids.

The more she thought about the molestation, her relationship with her mother as well as Girt molesting her gave her unbearable pain. That resulted in her getting high to ease the pain. When asked if they were ready to take a drug test Cinnamon and Nate would refuse, so DHS would automatically mark that down as a failed test. As far as getting her boys back, things weren't looking too good for the couple.

Nate decided to propose to Cinnamon and didn't put any effort to buy her a ring. He convinced her that it would be a better look in court if they were married. She was naive and desperate to the point where she would do anything to get regain full custody of her boys. Cinnamon stupidly agreed, and a few weeks later, they were husband and wife.

She continued to use drugs to dull her pain, but she made sure to attend N/A meetings on a daily basis. Nate on other hand decided that the meetings were not for him, so he stopped going. He also decided that he wasn't going to help pay any bills, and he made it loud and clear that he wasn't going to leave the drugs alone.

Cinnamon's back was against the wall; she was sick and tired of all the bullshit that was going on. Even though she was making visits twice a week with the boys it wasn't enough she wanted more.

She made the decision to clean herself up for her children's sake. She immediately called Tina to ask a few questions, one question in particular was about her leaving Nate and her proceeding with full custody without him. Tina advised her that it would not be possible. She stated that the children were removed from both parents, so therefore, both parents have to work together to get the children back.

Once Cinnamon heard those words, she was confused because that shit didn't make any sense to her. The next day, she called the Department of Human service and demanded the to speak to the supervisor.

She didn't tell the supervisor about the statement Tina made to her. Instead she discussed the fact that she wanted to proceed with obtaining custody without her husband. The supervisor then told her that she was not obligated to stay in any unhealthy relationship that she didn't want to be in.

Cinnamon began to reminisce on a day when she had visited the boys at mother's dearest house. Tina and mother dearest were laughing and joking around like they were best friends. Whether Tina knew it or not, mother dearest was manipulating her and turning her against Cinnamon. The Department of Human Services was only to be involved in the case for a year. After that the parent had to obtain a lawyer and proceed with the custody battle without the involvement of the Department of Human Services.

A year had passed, and the Department of Human Services closed the case. Cinnamon and Nate were not doing what was needed to obtain custody. Cinnamon was trying but not hard enough. She realized that if she stayed with her husband, she would never get full custody of her children.

The judge gave dual custody to mother dearest. He also stated that if anything happens to mother dearest, Cinnamon will have to answer to him.

She had a tough decision to make: it was either her kids or her husband. They were both the loves of her life. There were some women out there that would never separate from their husband, no matter the circumstances, death was the only departure. So who would Cinnamon have chosen—her husband or her kids?

CHAPTER 8

MUST GO

It was a gloomy cloudy Sunday afternoon when Cinnamon had blood gushing from the top of her head and a swollen lip. She and her husband got into a heated argument that eventually led to her getting her ass beat.

"I can't do this shit anymore!" she screamed". " I want out," she said to herself with snot pouring down her mouth.

Her kids were her world, and she would give her life for her two boys. She crunk up the car headed towards the trailer park where she and Nate lived.

"Let me see what they are playing on this fucking radio," said Cinnamon as she turnt on the car radio. Sam Cook's "*A change gone come*" was playing.

Driving home while listening to Sam Cook automatically made her feel at ease. It gave her a different outlook, it gave her hope and with that she was ready to stand up for herself. She was no longer going to play victim; she was going to fight to be a survivor.

She hopped out of the truck feeling confident especially after running out of the house and her husband Nate assuming she's going to suck

"DICK"

As Cinnamon approached the inside of the trailer, she opened the bedroom door and Nate was the first thing that her eyes saw. "You walked in at the right time!" he said excitedly, "Make me four hot dogs; I'm hungrier than a mother fucker."

Cinnamon rolled her eyes, walked to the kitchen and did what she was told. After putting the hot dogs on the stove, she realized how much exhaustion came from her being stressed, suicidal, and depressed.

She decided to take a hot shower while thinking about how she was going to get away from Nate and the baggage that came with him.

Maybe, I should sign him up with life insurance then kill him, so I can get the money and with the money, I can start a brand-new life. She was thinking all types of crazy shit until hot water relaxed her body enough for her to realize that murder was not an option. Her shower was rudely interrupted by Nate's loud-ass mouth as he yelled Cinnamon's name as loud as he could for her to bring him his fucking hot dogs.

"I swear this nigga gets on my damn nerves," she said as she turned the water off and stepped out of the shower. "Where are you? You better not be back there getting high!!" Nate yelled.

"Fuck you," she said as she almost slipped and busted her ass when she stepped out of the shower.

As she reached for the towel, she was shocked to see the bottle of Oxycodone pills sitting in the bathroom window next to her Dove Deodorant. She didn't want to kill her husband, the father of her kids, but she did want to get as far away from him as she could without him beating her ass. Giving him a good amount of pills will knock his ass out long enough for her to pack her shit and leave.

She put her plan into action and was ready to gain control over her life. She walked out of the bathroom, grabbed the sleeping pills, and headed towards the kitchen..

After making the hot dogs and placing them on a plate, her full attention was on the pill bottle. Cinnamon opened the pill bottle and poured six pills in the palm of her left hand. She then reached over to the left of her to grab a napkin.

"Okay, let's do it," she mumbled to herself while placing six pills on inside of the paper towel. She folded the paper towel three times and placed it on the kitchen counter. She then grabbed the screw-driver from the kitchen drawer, and banged on the pills until it was in powder form. She opened the napkin, and the first thing she noticed was how perfect the pills were crushed.

She poured it in the glass, and she filled the glass with with kool aid. She stirred up pills with a spoon for a few minutes. Afterwards she picked up the plate along with the glass of her special made kool aid and started to walk towards the room. She had to stop herself in her tracks because she was so nervous that her hands would not stop shaking.

"Get it together girl," is what she whispered to herself before entering the befroom. "Nate"!! Cinnamon yelled, while kicking the bottom of the bed. "Huh … what, what huh?" Nate mumbled as he jumped up like somebody just rang off 100 round shots into the ceiling. "Here is your food, baby," Cinnamon said with a gigantic smile on her face.

She handed him his plate along with the glass of ice-cold kool aid. He grabbed the plate first and the glass of kool aid second. Cinnamon got nervous again, so she grabbed a cigarette and lighter before leaving the room, and walking into the living room. "Okay, girl. it's done," she said to herself while sitting down on the couch to smoke her cigarette. How she was going to get out of her marriage was the only thing running through her mind at that moment.

Her second thought was the fact that she didn't have a dollar to her name. She also thought about how it would be for her to not see her kids for a while. Cinnamon hated that she had to leave them with mother dearest's bitch ass but she had no other choice; she had to get away from Nate.

If she stayed with him, she would never get full custody of her children. Cinnamon was sitting in a daze and didn't realize that her cigarette had burnt all the way out. "Damn," she annoyingly said to herself as she put what was left of the cigarette inside the ashtray.

She looked up at the clock that was in front of her and realized that twenty-five minutes had flown by like a bird. "Nate!" she yelled, as she rapidly jumped up off the couch and ran into the bedroom. As soon as she stepped into the room, her jaws dropped instantly at the sight of Nate's body hanging halfway off the bed. His head along with his right arm and right leg hanging off the bed touching the floor.

Beside his left hand, Cinnamon noticed the empty glass of kool-aid. That's when it became clear to her that Nate drank every last drop of that kool aid, and it's a possibility that he could be dead. Cinnamon heart started to speed at 100 beats per second.

"Oh, God. I can't go to jail for murder," she said to herself as she paced back and forth while shaking historically. "Wait, hold the hell up. How the hell is he dead if I only gave him four pills." That's when she decided to walk over to where he was and placed her hands over his forehead which seemed to be warm—so warm that he was perspiring.

She placed her hands over his chest to see if she could feel his heart beating. "Thank you, God," she said as she lifted her right hand off of his chest. Nate's body was functioning which means he wasn't dead. "Baby? Bae!!" She yelled, but Nate was non-reactive. She got no response from him whatsoever he was sleeping like a baby. She picked up her phone and Googled some numbers to a few domestic violence shelters. The first number on the list was located in Pearl, Mississippi an hour away from where she was. She dialed the number and a woman answered.

"Hello, this is the Safe and Sound Women's Shelter, Ms. Carver speaking, how may I assist your call?" she asked "Hello, my name is

Cinnamon, and I'm calling because I'm trying to get away from my abusive husband," Cinnamon nervously stated. "Okay, are you somewhere safe where you can talk?" "Yes, I can safely talk," Cinnamon humbly replied while looking over her shoulder. "I have a few questions to ask you, so let's get started" Ms. Carver happily said. "Where are you located?" Cinnamon was terrified of the thought of Nate waking up, and catching her on the phone. "I'm located in Port Gibson Mississippi" she replied.

"We are located in Rankin County, luckily we have available space, will you be bringing any children with you?" Ms. Carver asked. "I will be coming alone," Cinnamon sadly replied. "Okay, great. Can you come in today? If not, what's a good day for you?" And just to let you know, we don't hold beds for any individuals."

"I will be in Rankin County tomorrow, but where am I coming to?" Cinnamon asked. "Alright, well, all you have to do is go to the police department in Rankin County and give us a call when you arrive," said Ms. Carver. "Sure," said Cinnamon in her white girl voice to express how excited she was.

After hanging up the phone, she fell to her knees crying tears of joy. She humbly began to pray, "Dear Father, hallowed be thy name thy kingdom come thy will be done on earth as it is in heaven. Give us this day our daily bread and forgive us our trespasses as we forgive those who trespass against us. Lead us not into temptation but deliver us from evil for Thou is the kingdom, the power, and the glory for ever and ever. Amen. She then got up off her knees and immediately started to pack all of her belongings.

"Beep … beep … beep" was the sound of someone beeping their horn.

"Who in the hell is outside?" Cinnamon asked while peeking out of the window to see who was out there. "These messy mother fuckers," was what came out of her mouth as she watched mother dearest along with her three daughter's hop out of their car, and walked towards Cinnamon's front door "Boom, boom,

Was the sound of Nate's sister beating on the front door." "Nate, we need to talk to you," said mother dearest as she walked over to the living room window that was located beside the front door. She put her head to the window to take a look inside of the house.

"What do you see, Mama?" asked one of the daughters . "I don't see shit," replied mother dearest. "I know they are here because the navigator is in the yard. Don't worry, we'll be back later. Let's go y'all" she said to the three of her daughters while walking away from the trailer.

Cinnamon peeped out of her bedroom window and saw Dusty and the Dusters headed towards their car speeding away as if they were driving for NASCAR.

As Cinnamon stepped back, away from the window, she accidentally stepped on Nate's hand. She never moved him to the center of the bed because of the fear that he might wake up. She looked down and noticed that he didn't give any reaction when she stepped on his hand. *He is really knocked the fuck out,* she thought to herself, while moving him up in the center of the bed. *Okay, I gotta get out of here before mother dearest brings her nosy ass back here.*

After rambling through her closet all she found was three pairs of panties, two bra sets, no socks, five pairs of stretch pants and three shirts. She threw it all in a bag and headed out the back door. Her plan was to go to her uncle's house, so she could figure out a way to Pearl Mississippi.

As she got to the corner of her uncle's trailer, a blue Dodge Charger pulled up behind her. "Who the hell is this?" said Cinnamon as she slowly turned around to see who it was that was in the truck. Her eyes almost popped out of her socket once she realized who it was. She rushed over to the passenger side of the vehicle. "Yo." Where have you been bitch? China excitedly asked while rolling her eyes and snapping her fingers at the same time. China, who happens to be a gorgeous transsexual met Cinnamon at the chicken plant a while back. They became best friends working side by side on the assembly line pulling and plucking chicken.

China was loud and ratchet, and didn't take any shit from anyone, and I mean, anyone. When she talked, she use her hands and neck to get her point across.

Oh, and most importantly, her style was unique, and she never wore the same outfit twice.

"Girl, where the fuck you going with that cheap-ass Dollar store bag," China asked looking at Cinnamon from head to toe trying to figure out why she's looking a hot mess. "I'm so happy I ran into you," said Cinnamon, "I need you to take me to pearl." "What the hell for!?" China aggressively asked.

"Well, I'm leaving Nate for good. I'm going to go up against mother dearest and Claiborne County to get full custody of my children. First, I have to get the hell away from here, that's why you are driving me to Pearl," she said as she hopped in China's vehicle, and pulled the seat belt over her shoulders. "Let me stop and get some gas, then we will ride out," China told her as she pulled into the Shell gas station.

After she finished pumping the gas, she jumped in the car and sped towards the highway. Cinnamon and China laughed, joked, and talked about everyone that came to mind. The ride was an hour-and ten-minute ride, but they made it to the Pearl Police Department in exactly forty minutes.

"Well, you have arrived , bitch," China told her before she started to get emotional . "I'm proud that you decided to get your life back; it's about damn time you woke the hell up".Most people were afraid of China and thought she was a evil bitch. Only if they knew how sensitive and emotional she really was they would love her. China grabbed Cinnamon to give her one of the biggest hugs she had in a long time. "Call me once you get settled in babes," China told her before cranking up her vehicle and driving off..

Cinnamon took a deep breath before dialing the number to the domestic violence shelter. "Hello, my name is Cinnamon, and I was told to call this number once I arrived at the Pearl Police Department."

"Well, you just stay put, and someone will come to get you shortly. Be on the lookout for a white van."

After hanging up the phone, she looked around to see what was in the area. To the left of the police department was a gas station, to the right was an apartment complex, and that was all. A female police officer noticed Cinnamon standing close to the entrance. The officer approached Cinnamon and informed her that she could wait inside of the police department. Cinnamon looked at the officer, smiled and politely declined. Twenty minutes passed by, and an all-white mini-van pulled up in front of the police department.

"Are you Cinnamon?" asked an African—American woman who was sitting in the driver seat. "Yes," Cinnamon nervously stated before grabbing her bags that were on the ground beside her. Cinnamon walked to the side of the van, opened the door, threw her bags in the seat hoped in and closed the door. Gospel music was blasting through the radio, Marvin Sapp's "*The best in me*" was playing.

After the lady driving finished singing Marvin Sapp's song as if she was auditioning for American Idol she politely introduced herself. "Hello, my name is Diane," she said, "and I am the one who deals with the intake process." "Okay this is it," she said as she pulled into the driveway. The shelter was literally a three-minute drive away from the police department.

The shelter was nothing how Cinnamon pictured it; in fact, it was the total opposite. "Okay, just follow me," Diane told her as she exited the van, and walked into the house. The house was yellow and white, and so were the flowers that were perfectly lined up by the entrance.

Upon entering the building, Cinnamon and Diane walked between two double doors which lead to six offices. The first door had Diane's name on it. "Cinnamon, this is my office, and if you need me for anything you can find me here, come on in," said Diane as she unlocked the door to her office. She walked over to her desk, sat in the chair, and pulled some papers out of the desk drawer.

"Well, just don't stand there like a lost child, come have a seat," She jokingly said to Cinnamon while pointing to the empty chair that was in the front of her desk. Once Cinnamon sat down, Diane handed her some papers and a pen, "Okay, hun, fill those out while I discuss our terms and the different programs we offer," Diane told as she sipped from her bottle of water.

"This shelter is a "Safe Haven"for ninety days, and ninety days only". We offer assistance such as three months on rent and a first month's deposit, including the deposit to have the electricity turned on as well as furniture vouchers. You are allowed to cook your own meals, as long as you clean up after yourself. You will have a daily chore along with a 9:00 p.m. curfew. If you miss curfew, you will not be allowed back on the premises. We do have a 24hr smoking area out back for our residents who smoke. "Do you have any questions?" Diane calmly stated. I don't have any questions at the moment," said Cinnamon as she slid the set of papers towards Diane.

Diane looked over the paper, afterwards she placed them in a folder, and placed the folder inside of the drawer. Diane then stood up out of her chair and walked towards the door."Well, let me give you a little tour, grab your belongings and follow me," Diane told as she opened the door to her office, walked out and turned right.

"This is the kitchen," said Diane as she opened up the refrigerator. "As you can see, some of the girls here have their names on their personal belongings,". Cinnamon looked and notice a gallon of milk that had the name Yolanda written on it with a black marker. She followed Diane out of the kitchen which led to an enormous dining room . "This is the dining and television area It's open until 12:00 a.m." she said before pointing to her left.To the left of me is the shower room and towards the back is where the smoking area is located.

"Now, off to the grand finale," Diane stated as she headed towards this long hallway. She stopped in the middle of the hallway and stood in front of a wooden door. "Ookkkk,"Diane said before unlocking the door and walking inside the room.

"This is it," said Diane. " I will see you in the morning. You have a comfortable night," she told Cinnamon before she left out of the room, closing the door behind her.

"Well, this is it, girl," Cinnamon said to herself while taking off her clothes and getting into bed. She laid there looking at the window that was in front of her, thinking about her life without Nate and all the drama that came with him and his family.

Deep down, she feared Nate, and she was terrified of the thought of him finding

her. Only God could save Cinnamon if he did find out where she was. Cinnamon was anticipating the new journey of life that awaited her, and most importantly, her new life with her children who was now her main focus.

CHAPTER 9

THE BATTLE

"So, you're just going to leave me bitch, thinking I will never find you bitch huh?" Nate whispered into Cinnamon's ear while she laid in bed sleeping. He press his gun down a little harder on the right side of her cheek. Then he whispered in her ear a second time and said " I should blow your fucking head of bitch". Cinnamon jumped up and frantically started to scream. Nate placed his left hand around her throat, he placed the gun inside of her mouth and said " if you make another mother fucking word you're dead". Fear was written all over Cinnamon's face as she slowly nodded her head up and down in agreement.

She glanced over at the window that was located on the right side of her, and noticed that it was wide open. It was obvious that his entrance was her room window. "Want to know how I found you, hoe; I'm your fucking husband. I got a tattoo with your mother-fucking name on my fucking arm, bitch. I will always find you," Nate hollered as he cocked the gun back, and placed it in the middle of Cinnamon's forehead.

"Please don't do this, Nate. Think about the kids, honey," Cinnamon stuttered. Nate wasn't trying to hear it. "I love you, and if I can't have you, no one is going to have you," said Nate as he started to cry.

Cinnamon knew that her life was over, so she closed her eyes and started to pray. She knew he didn't come this far to talk, she knew he meant business. Nate aggressively kissed her on the lips and placed the gun back to her forehead. "Bitch I will see you in hell" is what he told her before pulling the trigger blowing her brains out.

Boom boom boom! Boom boom boom

Cinnamon quickly opened her eyes and realized that she was having a nightmare. She frantically sat up in her bed feeling puzzled.

At that very moment all Cinnamon could think about was how horrific her nightmare was, and more so how much it felt like reality.

Cinnamon got up out of her bed, grabbed a few of her things and went to the shower room to freshen up. Afterwards, she went to her room to pray. She kneeled down on the floor, closed her eyes, and held her head down. "Dear God, thanks a lot for putting me somewhere safe. Please continue to keep me safe, strong, and focused.

Father God, look after my kids, protect them, and cover them with the blood of Jesus, Amen." Cinnamon could feel the presence of the Holy Spirit. She got up off the floor and decided to write out a set of goals, short-term as well as long-term. Her short-term goal was to find a job, save money, get an apartment, and contact a lawyer. Her long-term goal was to gain full custody of her kids, and then they were going to get the hell out of Mississippi.

She also decided to find the nearest Narcotic Anonymous program.

Cinnamon got up to look in the mirror that was hanging on her wall. She told herself that today was going to be a good day. Then she did something that always made things a lot better: Music. She turned on the clock radio as loud as it could go. 50 cents' *Wanksta* was Playing.

Cinnamon sang along and danced in the mirror , "Damn, I'm juicy!!" she told herself as she popped, locked, and dropped it one last time before heading out the door to meet with Diane. She was filled with joy, and with that joy came a positive vibe, and she owed it all to music.

Walking towards Diane's office, she witnessed a Spanish lady sitting in the hallway talking to someone on her cellphone crying her heart out.. The lady had two black eyes, and a swollen lip. It was obvious that she had been beaten up pretty badly. Cinnamon knocked on Diane's door and walked straight in.

"Hello, Cinnamon, come have a seat, I promise I won't keep you too long," Diane politely told her. Cinnamon sat down in the chair and slightly glanced around the office. She smiled as she read some of the inspirational quotes hanging on the wall.

The office had a warm and comfortable vibe, with the aroma of a garden.

"Well, this meeting,I need you to come up with a set of goals",Diane said while placing a blank sheet of paper in front of Cinnamon, "What I need for you to do is write down three short-term goals, here's a pen," she said as she hands Cinnamon a black Paper Mate pen, but had no idea that Cinnamon was over prepared when it came to goal-setting.

Cinnamon just literally finished writing out some personal goals last night. Within the next 3 minutes Cinnamon was finished, and placed the sheet of paper in front of Diane. "Okay, let's see what you got," she told Cinnamon as she picked the paper up after putting on her glasses. "Number one is to get a job, number two is to save money, number three is to get in contact with a lawyer about regaining custody of your children."

"These are all great goals, Cinnamon, once you get employed, we will assist you with the first three months of rent and the deposit." "Are you serious!" said Cinnamon, not realizing how loud she was. She got up out of her seat and started to moonwalk or so she thought that's what she was doing Lol. "Okay, well, I see someone is super excited Diane told her as she laughed at Cinnamon's craziness.

"Hell yeah! Oops, my bad. I meant to say 'yes, ma'am. 'I am very excited," Cinnamon happily stated as she sat her ass down in her seat. "My goal is to be out of here in less than three months. " I forgot to mention that as of today I will be a student at Roman Trade College. I applied online and I chose the twelve week program for Dental Assistant". Diane congratulated her, handed her back the paper, and asked her to sign and date it. "Also, we will have a meeting every other Wednesday to check on your progress and see how far you've come on your list of goals, I'm proud of you" Diane told her. They gave each other a smile of approval, then Cinnamon left Diane's office feeling like a million dollars.

She was determined more than anything to get on her shit. The thing about Cinnamon is that she was a go-getter, and whatever she put her mind to, she did it without a doubt. She decided to go out for a little walk to get a feel of the neighborhood.

It was a different vibe in Rankin County no buses or trains you either walked cought a ride with someone or you had a car of your own. She spotted church's chicken not to far from the shelter and decided to check it out. She order a bite to eat and sat outside on the bench that was infront of the restaurant. "This is really good chicken," she said to herself, as she took a big bite of the juicy chicken. One thing about Cinnamon was that she had another addiction which was food.

For some strange reason, food took all her pain away. She would overindulge in eating until she passed out. As she swallowed the chicken and took a big sip of her orange soda, she noticed this older looking guy walking out of the chicken spot. There was something different about this guy. The first thing she recognized was his hair.

I mean anyone with eyes could see that he was a senior citizen but he had the most beautiful black curly hair anyone had ever seen. The second thing was his confidence and his "fuck with me I'll cut your throat" vibe.

The way he walked told Cinnamon everything she needed to know. The gold chain around his neck, his gold watch and rings told her that he had money.

He didn't notice Cinnamon sitting there, watching his every move. He was the perfect target plus she needed someone to drive her around to wherever she had to go. The small town she was in did not have any means of transportation, and Cinnamon was on survival mode.

"Hello, how are you doing? You don't look like you're from around here," Cinnamon said as she smiled at him flirtatiously. "No, I'm not. I'm actually from New York," he said as he smiled back. "Oh really, I'm from the Bronx, born and raised," she said excitedly. "I'm from Brooklyn, and my name is Levi. It's a pleasure to meet you."

"I'm running late but I would love to finish this conversation over dinner; take my business card, and call me some time," he said as he reached in his truck to grab the card. "I didn't catch your name, sweetheart," said Levi. "That's because I didn't give it to you," Cinnamon jokingly said before grabbing the card from his hand.

"Well, I think I'm going to like you, young lady," he told her as he got into his car, and drove off. Cinnamon looked down at the card which read 'Levi auto and care shop.' "Okay, then. Mr. Levi, I see you got it going on Zaddy," she mumbled to herself, as she placed the card inside of her back pocket.

"I wonder if this Church's chicken is hiring," she thought to herself while looking up at the big yellow "Church's Chicken" sign. She got up, walked inside and decided approached this young white girl who was behind the register for an application. The girl reached down underneath the register and handed Cinnamon what she asked for.

"Well, thank you," she said before sitting down to fill out the application. "Lord, if it's in thy will for me to get this job, I fully accept your decision," she muttered.

After filling out the application, she walked up to the front counter and asked to speak to the hiring manager. "Sure, give me one second," the young girl who resembled a country version of Kelly Bundy said. Then came a six-feet, slim built woman with loose-fitting khaki pants and a blue-collar shirt, with a name tag that read 'Manager' on it walking in Cinnamon's direction.

"Hello, I'm Lisa," she said as she walked up to Cinnamon. "Hi my name is Cinnamon, and it's a pleasure to meet you." Cinnamon handed her the application. "Looks like you came in at the right time because we are looking to hire a new team.

I see that your availability is open which is great. "I need you to come in on Thursday at 10:30 a.m. Make sure you have on some slip-resistant shoes. It was a pleasure meeting you, I'll see you Thursday," said Lisa before she walked towards the back of the restaurant. Cinnamon, who was feeling excited, got up and walked out of the restaurant, her destination was the shelter.

Speed walking across the street, all she could do was thank God because she knew that it was him who blessed her with the job. "Thank you, Lord. It's because of you that I just got blessed with this job. Father God, you told me to leave my husband, and I will receive blessings after blessings. I did exactly what you told me. I listened to that inner voice, and God blessed me. Thank you, Father."

By the time Cinnamon finished praising God, she was a block away from the shelter. Something stopped her in her tracks and landed her in front of this small sized building. That something told her to open the door and go inside, so she did. "Hello my name is Jay, and I am an addict," said this white guy with no teeth as he stood up to share his story.

"I've been on crystal math since I was twelve years old, overdosed over three times, and due to my addiction, I've been diagnosed with HIV. Thanks to God's grace, I've been sober for two years. My life has been a roller coaster, but as of today, I can honestly say I'm clean, and I'm happy. That's all I have to say, thanks for listening. He sat down, and beside him was where Cinnamon sat, and she was speechless because she never would have known that the guy was HIV positive. He looked like he weighed—over 300 pounds. Something in

Cinnamon's spirit advised her to stand up so she did. "Hello my name is Cinnamon and I'm an addict and because of this, I've lost custody of my children."

Cinnamon couldn't hold back the tears as she shared her story. "My kids are my world," she said as she grabbed the tissue from the guy with no teeth politely handed her.

"Thanks," she told him as she continued to talk, "my kids are my world and without them, there's no me; therefore, I'm here today to regain my sobriety. Thanks for listening," she said as she sat down in her seat. "Thanks for sharing," everyone else seated in that room said at the same time. It was something about that meeting that made Cinnamon want to keep going back, so she went faithfully, every day.

Not only that, but she was introduced to a sponsor for help with uncontrollable urges and emotional support. Cinnamon was committed to working and attending N/A meetings faithfully every day. Even though things were starting to look good, she began to feel lonely, she needed some attention, and decided to give Levi a call.

Ring Ring Ring

"Hello," said a voice on the other end of the phone. "Hello, is this Levi?" asked Cinnamon. "Yes, it is Levi. Who's this?" he asked. "This is Cinnamon, the girl from New York. We met at church's chicken spot like two weeks ago," said Cinnamon. "Oh, yes, the one with the beautiful big eyes. It took you long enough to call me, lil lady. You've been on my mind ever since we met and I would love to take you out to dinner."

"Okay, well. I love to eat; if you want, you can meet me at Kroger's, in a half an hour," said Cinnamon. "Make sure you wear something sexy; I want to show you off, baby," Levi jokedly stated. "I'll see what I can do my love see you few," is what she told Levi before hanging up the phone.

Cinnamon anxiously search her wardrobe to find something to put together. She came across this black dress she got from the donation rack at the shelter.

She slipped into her dress and decided to wear her heels; she was dressed to impress. As she left the building, a few girls were outside smoking cigarettes and couldn't help but to notice how beautiful Cinnamon looked as she walked across the street in her high heels. "Hey girl, you look good, girl," is what one of the girls told her. "I know, right?" Cinnamon jokingly responded appreciating the girl's compliment. approaching Krogers she noticed Levi standing beside his car looking very sophisticated and handsome.

When he noticed her coming towards his directions he swiftly walked around to the passenger side, opened the door, and waited for Cinnamon to enter into his newly bought car. Cinnamon was very impressed when Levi handed her a dozen roses.

When Cinnamon would make eye contact with Levi, she would notice that he had a big smile on his face as if he was honored to be in her presence.

As they walked into the restaurant they were greeted by a hostess who guided them to their table. Before the waitress could finish saying what she had to say,Cinnamon quickly asked for a margarita. She wasn't too ecstatic about being seen with a sixty-nine-year-old senior citizen as her date. There was something about him that had mysterious written all over him. That something made Cinnamon want to get to know more about him.

He had this aura about him that said 'play with me, and I'll fuck you up.' The waitress walked up with an ice-cold glass of Margarita. Cinnamon couldn't help but tell her how beautiful she was.

It was obvious that Cinnamon was extremely thirsty, anxious or nervous because she drank the entire glass of Margarita in one shot. "So, tell me a little bit about yourself Levi," Cinnamon quickly asked him, trying her hardest to take the attention off of herself and the empty glass of Margarita sitting in front of her. "You don't waste any time, huh baby?" Levi told her as he stared at the empty glass of Margarita.

"My wife passed away two years ago from cancer, and I've been alone for some time now. I'm looking for a "sweet little thing" like yourself that's going to love, and respect me.. I go to church every Sunday, and I also own a car dealership," said Levi as Cinnamon' is s eyes lit up. That's all he had to say to get her attention. Suddenly, she didn't feel creepy about being with a senior citizen.

One thing for sure God had always been in her corner mainly because there was no one else there. Cinnamon decided to take a chance and see what happens with this guy. Levi was a sweetheart, but it was somewhat obvious that he had a dark side to him.

For some strange reason, Cinnamon wanted to know more about his dark side more than anything. Months went on, and Levi was rocking hard with Cinnamon.

The following day Cinnamon walked into Diane office for their scheduled meeting.

"Hello, Cinnamon. I see that you're in a good mood,I'm sorry to interrupt but I have good news for you. The government is giving out grants to the shelters in the local area. Diane also informed Cinnamon that it would be a great idea to start looking for permanent residency.

Cinnamon couldn't believe her ears; her prayers had been answered and everything was working in her favor.

"OMG!! Thanks a lot, that's the best news I've heard in months," Cinnamon said. "You're welcome," Diane stated.

Cinnamon went into her room, and got on her knees to thank God for blessing her. *When you do what's right, good things start to happen,* she thought to herself.

She was crossing out all of her goals , one by one. The next goal was to get her boys back where they belong, which was with her.

CHAPTER 10

THE OFFICIAL

The sun was beaming, and it was a beautiful day,so Cinnamon decided to walk to work. She got stopped in her tracks when she heard someone beeping their loud as horn. *"Beep beep beep beep"*

"Hey, girl," Levi shouted, as he slowly drove up beside Cinnamon, continually beeping his horn like a mad man. Levi couldn't help but to notice how beautiful she looked as the sun hit her face.

"Oh, what's up handsome? Where are you coming from?" she excitedly asked as Levi pulled over to the left side of the street where she was standing.

Cinnamon reached into her back pocket and pulled out a blue and yellow hat that had church's written on the front., "I got a J-O-B," Cinnamon happily said as she danced her way into his truck.

"I'm actually on my way to work," She told him. "I was in the neighborhood and decided to sneak up on you,"said Levi. "Let me find out you are stalking me," she said as they locked eyes and smiled at each other.

Levi turned into the church's parking lot and quickly parked,"I can come pick you up from work if you like, sweetheart." Cinnamon looked at him with a light smile before saying, "That's okay, I'll walk. I can use the extra exercise. Thanks a lot for the ride, though. I'll call you later," she said as she got out of the car and closed the door. It was her first day at work, and she was super excited.

As she walked towards the entrance of her new job, she noticed Lisa the hiring manager standing in front of the entrance smoking a cigarette. "Hello, good morning," Lisa politely said as she held the door open for Cinnamon after tossing away the cigarette she was puffing on. Lisa's body language was a little off as if she was going through something.

"Okay, come here. Let me show you something," Lisa said as she faced the cash register, "this is how you clock in. You hit enter, then you enter the last four digits of your social security number, then hit exit, and you're all clocked in."

"Shantel!!" Lisa yelled, "Come show Cinnamon the ropes. I got work to do," she aggressively yelled before she walked into her office and slammed the door. "Shantel was an African—American, semi-boujee, and gorgeous. She was five-feet seven-inches tall, had a slim built and nicely shaped figure. "She's a bitch," Shantel whispered in Cinnamon's ear before giving Cinnamon a tour around the restaurant along with showing her how to work the register. She also gossiped about every employee, and I mean EVERY employee. She talked about Jenny who was at the register beside them. She told Cinnamon that Jenny had two kids by two different employees from the job.

Cinnamon made sure to make a note to not tell Shantel any of her personal business. Before she knew it, it was time to clock out. The day was done, and she actually enjoyed being at work.

"See you guys tomorrow," Cinnamon said as she walked out the doors and headed to the shelter. *Damn, it's hot out here,* she thought to herself as the sun beamed on every inch of her body.

Mississippi heat was no joke; it was 105°F, and she felt every bit of it. She finally made it to the shelter, and decided to take a shower. Perspiring made her feel dirty. After showering, she stretched out in her bed and no soon as she got comfortable and closed her eyes, she heard a loud bang on her door.

"Come in!" '' Cinnamon yelled as rudely as she could. She was exhausted and wanted to be left alone. "Ewww, someone is in a nasty mood" said Diane upon walking into the room. "No, I'm just tired," said Cinnamon as she laid her head back down on her pillow. "I have something you will be glad to have," Diane mentioned before placing a yellow envelope at the edge of her bed, and quietly walked out of the room.

Cinnamon glanced over at the envelope before dozing off. She must have been really tired because before she knew it, it was seven in the morning. "Damn I was out like a light," she whispered to herself once she realized how long she's slept. She glanced down at the envelope located at the end of her bed. Upon opening it and reading it, she couldn't believe that it was a letter stating that she qualified for rental assistance along with a voucher for an apartment. Three months on the rent and three months on the utilities. Cinnamon was overjoyed.

She put her game face on which meant that she was ready to do whatever it took to get her kids back. She decided to Google available apartments in the nearby area.

A few places popped up, so she decided to call the first one on the list. The location was not too far from the shelter, so she dialed the number.

"Hello, North Garden apartments," said this country ass guy over the other end of the phone. He had the stern voice of a country singer or a Texas Ranger. "Oh, hello. My name is Cinnamon, and I am calling about the two-bedroom apartment you have listed online."

"Yes, it's available. Why don't you come view the apartment today, and put in an application?" Cinnamon thought about it for a second before replying. "Sure, I will be there in twenty minutes".

"My name is Jimmy Earl, but you can call me Jim," he told her.

"Okay, see you shortly," Cinnamon happily responded.

She got off the phone and began to pray for God to take the wheel. Everything was in the Lord's control. She got dressed and took the fifteen-minute walk to the apartment complex. She felt this warm feeling come through her spine, sort of like a spiritual hug. It was at that very moment she knew a blessing was coming her way.

"*Knock knock knock*"

"Hello? Anyone here?" Cinnamon asked as she walked through the door, slowly smiling from ear to ear. As she entered the office, she noticed a guy standing up sipping on a cup of coffee while reading a newspaper. The aroma of cigarettes filled the entire office and lust filled this dude entire body when Cinnamon entered his office.

He rushed towards the door in an attempt to hold the door open for her, but he was a little too slow. As she walked towards the chair that was in front of his desk, he couldn't help but to gaze at her curves, as her hips shook left then to the right. The excitement of it all showed in the zipper part of his pants.

It kind of made Cinnamon feel a little uncomfortable especially when he asked her if she wanted to go up to view the apartment. It wasn't what he said; it was how he said it.

"Well, it's okay. I'm interested, so no need to view the apartment," Cinnamon nervously said as she replaced her facial expression with an odd smile. "Are you sure, honey?" Jimmy asked while touching Cinnamon's right hand. Cinnamon almost threw up because the sight of his teeth made her sick. Half of them were gone, except for the top three and bottom three. It was clearly obvious that they were hanging on by a thread.

"I'm sure, Jimmy. I'll take your word that the apartment is in good shape." Her instinct told her to not take her ass upstairs, and she did just that. "I will need your signature on all these forms, and I also have some paperwork for the shelter to sign," said Jimmy. Cinnamon was super excited because at that very moment, her prayers were answered.

She was one step closer to getting her kids back where they belong, with their mother. After filling out all of the paperwork, she headed back to the shelter. Cinnamon couldn't wait to get out of Jimmy's office; he made her feel very uneasy . She rushed over to the shelter as fast as she could to share the good news with Diane.

Cinnamon spotted Diane exiting the premises about to head home. "I was looking for you, young lady," Diane told her before unlocking her car door. She reached down in her purse and handed Cinnamon a card with a lawyer's information on it. "She's one of the best attorneys in Mississippi; she'll be expecting your call," .

OMG, thanks. I have some good news as well," said Cinnamon as she opened the passenger side door and sat down on the passenger seat of Diane's car. "I found a two-bedroom apartment, and here's the paperwork," Cinnamon said as she handed her the paperwork.

"Monday morning, when I come in, I would like to have a sit down with you, so we can go over everything, oh and make sure you don't miss any of your N/A meetings." Diane told her as she put the keys inside the ignition.

Cinnamon opened up the passenger side door and stepped out, she looked Diane in her eyes and told her that she appreciated everything. Cinnamon decided to attend the four o'clock N/A meeting which was in the next ten minutes.

Upon walking through the doors, a load of smoke smacked her dead in her face. One thing about these meetings, the majority of the members smoke cigarettes and drank coffee back to back. She grabbed a cup of coffee, sat down and joined the conversation.

"Hello, everyone. My name is Cinnamon, and I'm an addict" "Hello, Cinnamon," the crowd said as she stood up to share with the group. "I've been on every drug that you can name to try to ease the pain that lives in the middle of my chest, but nothing worked," said Cinnamon as she began to get emotional. "After my high went away, the pain would appear and the cycle repeated itself over and over again. I have to beat this thing, I can't let it get the best of me," Cinnamon said as she sat back down in her seat. The crowd thanked her for sharing her story. The meeting lasted an hour and a half. Afterwards, Cinnamon went to the shelter, took a bath, prayed, and fell asleep.

The next day, she went to work, attended the N/A meeting, and then, to bed. That was her everyday routine. Monday crept up on her so fast that she couldn't hide the excitement. Cinnamon woke up early on Monday morning, super ready to contact the lawyer.

"Ring ring ring"

"Hello, this is Strafford Law Firm, my name is Ms.Stratford, how may I help you?". "My name is Cinnamon, and I'm looking for help to regain custody of my children." "How many children do you have?" asked Ms. Stratford. "I have two boys ages four and seven," said Cinnamon. "With who are your children living with?, and how long have they been out of your custody?" Cinnamon took a deep breath before answering "They have been with their grandmother for a year and a half." "Are you employed; do you have a stable place to live?" Ms. Stanford asked. "Yes, yes, and yes," Cinnamon said. "Great, I'm going to email you some forms to fill out and sign. I will need a list of all the documents listed in the email," said Ms. Stratford. "OMG, thanks so much, "Cinnamon happily said. "Great, so what's your email address," Ms. Stanford asked. Cinnamon told her the email address.

"Check your email in about ten minutes; once you fill out the forms, we will then take it from there." Cinnamon stood up and started to moonwalk to her room, singing Michael Jackson's "*You no I'm bad I'm bad come on*" she sang to herself as she opened the room door. She threw herself on her bed and stared at the ceiling.

Diane walked in a few minutes behind her, "I have some news for you, hun. The director approved your application for an additional three months on the rent. Did you contact the lawyer?" Diane asked. "Yes, I did, and she agreed to take my case," Cinnamon replied. "Great, so let me go finish your paperwork,"Diane told her as she walked out of the room as if she was late for a meeting. Cinnamon was overwhelmed with excitement, so she decided to take a nap. She fell into a deep sleep; her body was so relaxed that she began to drift off into a dream, a dream that seemed familiar.

"I'm from Chicago, bitch. You don't want any of this," Dee Dee said, as she patted on her chest as if she was King Kong. Cinnamon just looked at her while taking a hit of crack. Next thing you know, her eyes looked as though they were ready to pop out of the socket.

Cinnamon stood up and ran to the window to see who was trying to break into the house; she was obviously paranoid, and hallucinating "Shhhhhh!" she whispered to Dee Dee as she ran to make sure the door was locked.

"Bitch ain't no mother fucker out there. I been with your mother-fucking uncle for ten years," Dee Dee said as she put the lighter to the pipe.

Cinnamon jumped out of her sleep, sweating like she just ran a twenty-mile marathon. She was so scared and terrified that she fell to her knees to pray to God. "Dear God, do not let me go back to that lifestyle. Take away the smell and the urge of all drugs. Amen."

She got up, took a deep breath, and then laid back down in her bed. Two weeks went by when Cinnamon got a knock at the door. Suddenly Diane rushed in and said, "I got good news for you. Your apartment was approved, and you will be signing your lease today!!" yelled Diane, in the most exciting voice ever heard. "OMG! I can't believe it. Everything is falling into place, thanks to God," Cinnamon said after hugging Diane, and almost squeezing her to death.

"I need you to come to my office as soon as possible to fill out some paperwork. Cinnamon did exactly what she was told, and within one week, Cinnamon was in her apartment. Three weeks passed before Cinnamon heard back from her lawyer.

She received a letter in the mail that informed her that she will be standing in front of a judge in the next two months for a custody hearing. Cinnamon had two months to line all of her ducks in a row. She continued to work, and as far as schooling went, her graduation was in six months.

If the judge granted her full custody, her kids would be able to witness their mother walking on a stage to receive her certificate as a Dental Assistant. Cinnamon was extremely anxious about finally going to court.

Levi was still providing and supporting her each and every day. Cinnamon couldn't get rid of him even if she tried. He helped her furnish the entire apartment, from top to bottom.

Levi made a promise to Cinnamon that no matter what, he will help her get her boys back home where they belong. Even if it meant taking matters into his own hands. He told her this while lifting up his shirt revealing a pistol.

Levi finally showed Cinnamon a glimpse of his dark side. The look in his eyes screamed "Murder murder kill kill". When Levi and Cinnamon were together she would notice how Levi would be dazed out in deep thought. His persona told Cinnamon that he carried a deep ruinous past.

Levi was falling really hard for Cinnamon, so hard that he was willing to take someone else's life in order to please her. With this information, Cinnamon stored it in the back of her head just in case it was needed. Mother dearest was not going to win this war. She might have won the battle, but the war was going to be won by Cinnamon. Period.

CHAPTER 11

"THE STORY OF LEVI"

It was the winter of 1994 in Bronx, New York,and for the past two weeks Levi has been stalking this bank manager, keeping tabs on his daily routine, and work schedule.

Levi knew what time the manager arrived at work, what time the shift changed.

Levi knew that the manager whose name is Joel Rivera along with a female bank teller by the name of Rolanda Ellis arrived at the bank every morning at 7:45a.m.

Levi was no rookie at robbing banks it was like a walk in the park. Most importantly Levi never brought anyone with him, he was alone. His favorite quote is that " If he got caught he knows for a fact that he's not telling on himself ".

Levi also knew that around 8:30a.m every day except weekends, three more bank tellers would arrive. Two bank security guards would arrive at 8:45, and at 9:00 the bank would open for business.

After mastering his plan to perfection it was now time to put his plan into action.

It was 7:44 am the bank teller Rolanda Ellis arrived on time like clockwork.

Levi hopped off his motorcycle and started walking across the street to the bank.

He slowly crept up behind Rolanda and pressed his gun to her lower back.

"Don't you fucking say a word keep moving" said Levi ass he shoved her inside the bank.. "Please don't kill me" she cried intensively terrified of what Levi could be capable of doing to her.

Once he was inside of the bank, he glanced up at the oversized clock hanging on the wall to his left and realized that he only had ten minutes before the surveillance cameras automatically turned on.

"Give me all of the fucking money," Levi shouted, after he wrapped his hands viciously around her throat with full force. He then

Ordered her to unlock the volt, and she did exactly what she was told.

After she unlocked the volt Levi slammed her on the floor as hard as he could, and threatened to blow her head off if she moved.

Levi quickly grabbed a garbage bag that was on top of the small garbage can beside the volt.

He filled the bag up with as much money that he could get inside.

Afterwards he looked over at the female teller and realized that she was not laying on the floor. Levi glanced around the bank,"I got that bitch ," Levi shouted after hearing the teller tripping over something and falling to the floor. Levi quickly ran toward the direction where the sound came from. "Yea that motherfucker going to die today; you just fucked up," Levi angrily stated.; "I am fucking King Levi—do or die," he said as he ran to the back of the bank looking for the bank teller who was trying to escape.

When he turned the corner by the exit, he caught sight of the teller, who was on the floor, holding her ankle. Levi could notice the phone cord in front of the bank teller. "Hello, mother fucker," said Levi as he held up the gun to the teller head pulling the trigger.

Boom Boom

He shot twice, blowing the right side of the bank teller's face off.

Levi's eyes widened at the sight of the teller's scattered brains, and facial pieces filled with blood as it landed all over the wall. Levi paused for a few seconds feeling superior and fearless..

It was as if Levi got a natural high from taking someone's life. He quickly bounced back to reality,grabbed the bag filled with money, and headed towards the back of the bank.

Levi had to get the fuck out of there, so he ran out the back door, hopped on his motorcycle, and left without being seen by a soul.

He mastered the whole plan from A to Z. Levi was a genius and very intelligent. The bank that he'd looted was located in the South Bronx. He knew the cops were looking for a man on a motorcycle in New York City. Therefore Levi stashed his getaway car in Newark, NJ.

He was planning on leaving the state with a whole new identity. He pulled into the garage, and parked his bike all the way to the back of the garage beside a black car with tinted windows.

He quickly opened the driver side door of the black Mercedes Benz. Threw the bag of money in the back seat and crunked the car up.

Levi's wife Pattie was in the passenger seat nervously waiting for him the entire time, and couldn't stop hugging him and kissing him like a psycho woman. Levi and Pattie relocated to Jackson Mississippi, bought a big beautiful house and started a Cleaning business. He snatched a total of $347,000 from the bank heist and enjoyed every penny of it.

Three years later his wife was diagnosed with stage 3 breast cancer, a month later she passed away. Levi was devastated, it's been seven years since her death, but to him it felt like yesterday. Cinnamon made him feel how he felt when he met his wife for the first time. He was falling hard for her; she meant everything to him, and he would do anything to prove his love, even if that meant he had to take someone's life.

CHAPTER 12

COURT

"Hey girl, this Levi, I'm on my way to come get you. I'll be there in twenty minutes, so make sure you are outside." "Damn, I ain't going to have time to do my makeup, but okay I'll be outside."

Cinnamon hated to be rushed, but she couldn't complain because Levi was driving her sixty miles to attend her custody hearing for free. Twenty minutes felt like five, and before she knew it, Levi was blowing up her phone. "Lord, humble me and guide me, so that I can do thy will Amen."

After praying, Cinnamon grabbed her purse and phone while running out of the shelter like she was running for her life. Once outside the premises, Cinnamon noticed Levi's red pick-up truck parked down the block. While walking to the truck, she felt this wave of positive energy flow through her body.

The feeling was like waves calmly flowing through the ocean. As chills fluttered her body, Cinnamon couldn't help but to think that it was nobody but the Lord comforting her. *Prayer works,* she thought to herself as she opened the passenger side door of the truck.

Once inside, Levi was bobbing his head up and down while listening to the infamous Jackie Wilson's , "*Lonely Teardrops.*" "I tell you, no lie, Jackie Wilson has one of the best voices. Cinnamon fell in love with his voice the very first time she heard him sing on TV when she was eleven-years-old.

His voice was magical, there's no debate about it. Your heart and soul will drift away while his voice travels through your body turning you oblivious to any stress and pain. "I see you got good taste in music," said Cinnamon, as she hit the volume button to turn the music up. "Why are you staring at me like that?" she asked, as Levi looked at her with love in his eyes. He was falling for Cinnamon and he was falling hard. Cinnamon on the other hand wasn't thinking about love at all.

Her primary focus was regaining custody of her children; anything else besides that had to take a back seat. The whole ride there, they listened to Jackie Wilson and The Temptation, then out of nowhere, Levi decided to ask Cinnamon a question that has never crossed her mind, a question that she hasn't given any thought of.

"So girl, are you prepared mentally if the judge makes the decision to give full custody to the grandparents?" If looks could kill, Levi would have been as good as dead. "Over my dead body, and I mean that sincerely," Cinnamon said.

They gazed each other in the eyes for a few seconds. Levi knew that Cinnamon meant what she said. The expression on her face was clear as day. Murder and homicide was going to be the case they gave her because she was going to kill for what belonged to her, point blank, and then the period.

"Well, I'm here for you, baby girl, through the good and the bad. I'm here," Levi said as he lifted his shirt up revealing his 38 snub nose revolver on the right side of his hip securely tucked inside of his pants. He taped it twice before letting his shirt down.

Cinnamon knew what the vibe was, she knew Levi would kill for her and wouldn't think twice about it.

"Welcome to Port Gibson" was the large sign they passed as they entered into Claiborne County. For some estranged reason, Cinnamon couldn't keep her heart from speeding as they drove down Hwy 61. She began to think about the seven years she wasted while residing in that county.

The truth is while living in Mississippi she lost herself. She forgot who she was, she forgot about her street knowledge and everything she learned while growing up in the Bronx. That's the reason she smoked crack; she was lost alone, and wanted to die Just like the majority of people in poverty whom suffer from mental illness and who are victims of mind control. African Americans who don't know who they truly are carry around vicious anger towards one another, but mainly on themselves, sometimes unknowingly. Until we do our research on the history of our ancestors we will continue to be mentally enslaved. Living in the matrix controlled by the same people who brought our ancestors to America.

All the while keeping us blinded with deceitfulness, and using the celebrities as puppets to hinder us from the truth.

Cinnamon was not exempt, she was lost, she hated herself, she was blind until the most high sat patiently beside her through the tough times. .

Levi pulled up to the courthouse, and looked at Cinnamon before saying "Well lady, I will be right here, waiting on you," Levi lustfully told her as he admired how beautiful she looked.

Cinnamon made sure she looked extra fabulicious mainly because she had a point to prove. She hopped out and walked across the road like she was auditioning for America's Next Top Model.

As she walked up the stairs and into the courtroom, The first face she noticed was Nate, she couldn't help but to roll her eyes as far back in her head as they would go.

"Oh so you can't speak to your husband now? Oh, I see how it is, wifey," Nate sarcastically told her as he stood in the entrance of the court house. Cinnamon politely walked past him like he didn't exist.

"Hello Mrs. Cinnamon, how are you today?" Her lawyer asked with a big, bright kool-aid smile on her face after watching Cinnamon give Nate the cold shoulder.

Her lawyer was a slim, African—American, middle-aged, light-skinned woman. She had a warm and calm spirit filled with positive energy. Cinnamon stood beside her and said I'm feeling really anxious. all I want is my kids home with me." "Well we did everything that was required, so let's calm down, Cinnamon," her lawyer calmly told her as she gently patted Cinnamon on her shoulder. They walked into the elevator and landed in the waiting area. Her Lawyer advised her to take a seat and informed her that the judge will be out shortly.

She could see mother dearest and her husband sitting in the rear of the courtroom.

Cinnamon decided to sit three rows in front of them. Things couldn't get any uglier because within a couple of minutes, Nate walked in and sat in the same row four seats down from her.

"Fucking goofy," said Cinnamon as she watched Nate sit there looking like he was the man of the year foh . The sight of his face made her nauseous.

Not long after Nate walked in, the judge walked out and everyone stood up. "This court is in session docket number 99877655 in the custody hearing of Cinnamon vs The Department of Human Services. You may be seated," said the security guard.

While everyone sat down, Cinnamon could see her lawyer waving her hand telling Cinnamon to come sit up front closer to her. Cinnamon didn't hesitate; she did exactly what she was told. Her lawyer looked at her, gave her a smile and a pat on her shoulder, she could see how nervous Cinnamon was.

"Judge, we are here today because my client wishes to regain full custody of her children. A year ago, you granted temporary custody to their grandmother and grandfather. My client has relocated, got a job, and an apartment. She also has six-months worth of random drug screening."

"With that being said, my client wishes to regain full custody of her two children. To Cinnamon's surprise the case workers from The Claiborne County Department of Human Services were in court as well.

Later on, Cinnamon found out that the judge requested for them to be present . "Okay, that's great to hear, but I will need more than these documents to determine if your client is going to regain full custody of her kids. The judge turned to his left to face the caseworkers. "I will need y'all to go view and take pictures of the apartment."

"Court will resume in ninety days," the judge said as he banged his gavel down as hard as he could. Disappointment was written all over Cinnamon's face seconds before becoming enraged.

She thought for sure that she would be bringing her kids back home with her. Unfortunately, she thought wrong. "It's okay, you're going to get your kids back. Don't worry," her lawyer told her as she tried her best to make Cinnamon feel better.

Cinnamon looked over at mother dearest who was sitting over there looking like tweety-birds grandma with those oversized glasses, damn near bigger than her face.

Cinnamon fought the thought as well as the urge to walk over there and choke the shit out of her. Instead she stood up Out of her chair, gave her Lawyer a hug goodbye and angrily headed towards the exit. Mother dearest was standing by the elevator with this little smirk on her face.

"I can't stand that bitch," Cinnamon said to herself while opening up the passenger side door of Levi's truck.

"Are you okay? what's wrong?" he asked. "That damn judge wants to see for himself how the house looks so he asked the social workers from to make a home visit," Cinnamon narrated. We are scheduled to come back to court in ninety days!"

Levi grabbed the both Cinnamon's hand and told her "I know that you are upset but trust me everything will be okay," Levi hated to see Cinnamon upset. He knew how much her kids meant to her.

"Let's go grab a bite to eat. I can use a good meal right about now," he stated while cranking up his truck and headed towards the highway.

They pulled up into his favorite Chinese buffet upon arriving in Jackson. They walked inside and were seated by one of the waitresses. After being seated, Cinnamon watched two little boys who were around the same age as her boys playing with their toy trucks.

She couldn't stop the tears from falling from her eyes as she hopelessly watched the boys interact with their mother.

She got up and ran into the ladies room crying uncontrollably.

She sat on the toilet and cried her eyes out not realizing that someone walked in the restroom witnessing her mental breakdown. Feeling sympathetic the lady who entered the restroom knocked on the bathroom stall and said "Excuse me, are you okay? Feeling startled Cinnamon said Yes, I'm fine, thanks,"

Filled with embarrassed she waited until the lady exited the restroom, before got up off the toilet and walked by over to the table where she was seated.

Cinnamon and Levi sat there, ate, laughed and talked for about three hours. Levi had a way of taking her mind of negative energy.

Three weeks later, the case worker was scheduled to come make a home visit. Cinnamon heard someone knocking at the door. "Coming!!!" she yelled as she ran out of her room to the front door.

"Hello Cinnamon, I'm here on a court order to view the apartment," the case worker said as if Cinnamon didn't already know this. "Well, come on in and let me give you a grand tour." She jokingly said to the two ladies as they entered her apartment "This is the boys room, my oldest will get the bottom bunk and my youngest will be on top," she said as she pointed to the bunk beds.

Nice, I love the sponge bob sheets," she said as she pulled out a camera, and snapped three pictures of the room.

Afterwards she took numerous of the remaining of Cinnamon's fully furnished two bedroom apartment.

. Before leaving, the case worker gave Cinnamon a fake speech on how proud she was of her accomplishments.

Cinnamon wasn't trying to hear it though she knew it was bullshit.

Time flew by extremely quick, and before Cinnamon knew it, it was time to go back to court for the second time . Cinnamon knew for a fact that this was it; this would be the day that her boys will permanently be in her custody. The judge required her to take a random drug test every week, get a job, and permanent place to live.

Cinnamon achieved all the necessary requirements. To top it off she brought proof to show that she was in school for Dental Assistant. Levi didn't hesitate when Cinnamon asked if he would drive her to Court. Levi made plans for them to go to a water park the following weekend. He wanted to do something nice to welcome them back home.

"Well, this is it, baby girl. I'll be right here when you come out." Cinnamon stepped out of the truck and walked across the street to the courthouse. She was super excited and proud of herself. She couldn't wait to see the expression on mother 's dearest face when the judge award her custody of her boys.

When she walked into the court room she saw the two caseworkers, district attorney, and mother dearest, all huddled together, having a conversation. Her lawyer waved at her to come and sit next to her so she started to walk in that direction. "What the hell are they talking about?" she asked as she sat down next to her lawyer.

I don't know that's not my concern. My concern is you." Cinnamon looked at her and smiled. She then realized that her lawyer was a cool, calm, and collective woman, and at that moment, she realized that she really liked this lady.

"All rise. Docket number 67906543 in a custody hearing for Cinnamon vs The Department of Human Services," the security said. The judge walked out and after sitting down, he told everyone to take a seat.

The judges looked at the caseworkers and asked "Okay, first I would like to know if you visited Cinnamon's apartment and what evidence you have to back it up?" "Yes, your honor. I have taken a trip to her apartment and photos of the entire apartment have been taken. We have those pictures here if you would like to see them," said one of the caseworkers.

"Can you grab those for me, John?" said the judge as he looked to the left of him at the bailiff who was standing there like a statue. "No problem, sir," said John as he walked over to the table where the case worker was sitting. She handed him a folder with papers in it. As the judge opened the folder, Cinnamon turned around to take a glance at the expression on mother's dearest face.

As she turned around, it seemed like mother dearest was thinking the same thing because she locked eyes with her instantly.

The judge had an aura as if he was surprised by Cinnamon's accomplishments. When she left Port Gibson, no one thought she would come back with a bang. They were wrong, and they underestimated her strength, that's for damn sure.

"Okay, so I'm looking over everything, and there is something here that doesn't add up," the judge said. *Here we go with the fuckery,* Cinnamon thought to herself. She wanted to jump up and be ratchet, but decided not to besides that would only make things worse.

Your lease shows that the total amount of rent is $595 a month. Then there's a light bill every month, water bill phone bill, and household supplies. Your total income per month by the looks of your check stubs isn't enough to pay for your finances let alone two children.

Judge, may I address the court?" requested Cinnamon's lawyer. When he shook his head up and down she began to speak. "Judge, I understand what you're saying, but we have to considered the fact my client is working two part time jobs while attending college."

"Yes, but you don't understand that having two children is a big responsibility. I have to be sure that if her kids return to her they will have stability."

He looked over at the caseworker and asked if they had anything to add. "As a matter of fact, we do your honor. "We would like to request a hair sample for drug screening. We want to make sure that Cinnamon is 100 percent sober and free of any narcotics."

Cinnamon could hear mother dearest and Nate back there running their big mouths, but decided not to say anything because again it wouldn't be a good look for her.

"I agree, so with that being said, we will return in ninety days. I'm requesting your client to bring the hair sample as well proof that she will be able to financially support her children," the judge said. Well judge, my client isn't the only parent. they also have a father who is required to financially provide for them as well. Not only that, but your honor, should he not be required to submit to a drug screening as well?" the lawyer questioned.

"Nate, do you have anything to say?" "Yes, judge. If you don't mind, I have something I would like to say. Well judge, I give up all rights. I'm not in any position to even think about regaining custody," said Nate.

"Does that answer your question?" the judge asked as he grabbed his gavel while looking at Cinnamon's lawyer. He banged it down like he was trying to break a rock into a million pieces. "This case will continue in ninety days."

Cinnamon couldn't decide if she wanted to smack her lawyer, the judge, that caseworker or smack the hell out of mother dearest's snaggle mouth ass.

"This some fucking bullshit!" Cinnamon angrily yelled as she jumped out of her seat and stormed out of the courthouse.

Nate got up and followed her to the elevator. He had to try to see where her head was at. "I miss you, wifey," he slowly whispered in her ear. "Get the hell away from me. I'm not falling for your manipulations, Nate so get the hell away from me." Cinnamon felt ambushed and disgusted, so when the elevator door opened, she rushed to get inside. She couldn't stand the thought of being too close to Nate. Before the elevator door closed she mentioned one last thing to Nate "Oh, and by the way, your mother is going to wish she never met me, mark my words". Levi could tell by the look on her face that it didn't go well.

"I want her dead. I want her fucking dead," said Cinnamon as she got into Levi's truck. "What happened? Baby calm down and talk to me," Levi told her. Cinnamon looked him in his eyes before asking a question. "You said you love me and you would do anything for me right?" "RIGHT?!! Cinnamon frustratedly yelled.

Levi nodded his head in agreement and calmly said "I'll do anything for you, my love, just tell me what you want, and your wish will be granted."

"I want that old bitch DEAD!!!!" Yelled Cinnamon.

Cinnamon was tired of being played for weak, it was time mother dearest got what she deserves. It was time she met her maker. She messed with the wrong one, and it was time she pay for it.

"Levi reached into the glove department, and pulled out his 38 snub nose revolver.

He was ready to shut this little town the fuck down. He was a beast, you know the type of beast who was so good at what he did that he never got caught.

Within a matter of seconds he transformed into a monster, better yet a killer. The look in his eyes was pure evil and demonic . "I'm on it; today I will prove my love to you." Just stay right here and keep the truck running. Don't leave this truck, understand?" asked Levi before opening the passenger side door and exiting his truck.

"Yes, I understand," she said as she watched his walk towards the courthouse with his gun in his hand. Cinnamon's stomach started to turn flips, and she felt nauseous.

Something horrible was about to happen and she had to ask herself if she was sure about what she was asking Levi to do for her. Will she be able to mentally and physically handle the consequences of killing her children's grandmother?

CHAPTER 13

MURDER WAS
THE CASE

Cinnamon opened the door to the truck so fast that she broke a nail. "Damn it," she shouted as her finger began to throb in pain. She then ran across the street; she didn't know she could move as fast as she did. She had to catch up to Levi before he pulled that trigger.

Killing mother dearest in public wasn't a smart move. If caught, Cinnamon would be charged with first-degree murder, and she would never see her kids again. That was why she had to stop him, so they could figure out a better way to get rid of mother dearest for good.

As she turned around the corner, she saw Levi slowly creeping behind mother dearest and her husband's vehicle. Cinnamon almost pissed on herself as she witnessed him lifting up his shirt. She began to run at full speed until she finally caught up with him.

"Levi not now, let's go. We got to go," she said as she grabbed him by the arm. The look in Levi's eyes was horrifying; it was like he was possessed. Cinnamon grabbed his arm and led him to his truck. Once inside, they sat in silence for about ten minutes before Levi decided to speak. "So, tell me something Cinnamon, why the hell did you stop me? " he said in a scary, but sexy demonic voice.

"I thought about it, Levi, If we do it right here in front of the courthouse where there are police officers and witnesses all around the premises, we will be shot dead where we stand," said Cinnamon.

"We are smarter than that Levi, now crank up and let's go, so I can tell you how I'm going to turn mother dearest lights out." Instead of taking Highway 61, they decided to take Highway 18 which was the back way to Jackson Mississippi.

"So what's the plan, love?" asked Levi, "I was thinking that you can sit this one out; I will be the one to blow her brains out." Levi looked at her and thought to himself of how his demonic ways were rubbing off on her. She was turning him on, and he loved it, especially when she would clap her hands and talk at the same time.

Truth was, she wasn't thinking straight. The stress of this case was wearing her down. She was emotionally unstable and desperate, desperate enough to kill for her children.

When you are in the presence of wicked and demonic people for a long period of time, some of their ways will rub off on you. Demonic forces are real. Be careful who you spend your time with.

"The plan is, you're going to drive to Port Gibson in the middle of the night. I will sneak into the house and into her bedroom, and put the lights out for her ass," said Cinnamon. "You have to make sure that you are ready to pull off as soon as you see me coming out of the house.

I will grab the boys out of bed and run out to the truck. I'm going to get my kids back one way or the other". Cinnamon told him this while adding in Rankin County.

Levi pulled into the apartment complex where Cinnamon resided. After he turned the engine off, Cinnamon gave him a kiss on the cheek. "Levi, I want you to know that I appreciate everything you've done for me. I could not have done this without you," she told him. Levi just sat there with a huge kool-aid smile on his face."

"Once I figure out the layout of my plan, you'll be the first to know. I'm going to go upstairs to take a hot shower; I'm exhausted." She got out of the car and walked up the stairs to her apartment. Walking into her apartment, she couldn't hold back her tears as it began to pour down her face. After closing the door and locking it, she broke down and proceeded to cry uncontrollably . "Why god, why?" she shouted as she fell to the floor, and cried herself to exhaustion.

She cried about her entire life as a whole. From the beginning, when she was taken away from her mother, being sexually and physically abused. From the prostitution, homelessness, all the way to her drugs of choice. She cried for her part in this whole situation, like ignoring all the signs that were shown to her by God.

She should have left Nate a long time ago but she couldn't, she was too weak. The truth is everything she was going through was all her fault. She forgot who she was and where she came from and didn't have a clue about where she was going.

She slowly picked herself up and headed for the shower. Taking off her clothes and stepping into the shower automatically puts her in relaxed mode. She felt like a brand-new woman. Once she was done showering, she decided to lay down and rest.

As she laid in her bed, she gazed up at the ceiling thinking about everything that happened today at court. She also had to come up with the exact date and time she was going to visit mother dearest.

She was so relaxed that she drifted off into a deep sleep. She woke up the next day feeling like a new person. The first thing that was on her agenda was scheduling that appointment for the drug screening. "Hello, my name is Cinnamon, and I'm calling about the hair drug testing. I would like to set an appointment as soon as possible."

"Great!! You actually called right after someone canceled their appointment. If you like, you can come in today at 2:30 p.m." "Yes ma'am!! I will definitely be there," Cinnamon hung up the phone and called in to work to inform them that she would be running a little late. Her job came first regardless of the circumstances.

Pulling up at the clinic, Cinnamon was anxious to get the process over fast and in a hurry. "Hello, my name is Cinnamon, and I'm scheduled for 2:30 p.m."

"Okay, great! Well, fill this form out and the doctor will be with you shortly." Cinnamon was extremely curious to know how much hair they were going to remove. "Cinnamon, can you follow me please?" asked a white nurse who led Cinnamon behind two double doors.

As they walked to the back, the nurse led her into a room. "Sit here and take your hair out for me, and I'll be back in a few seconds." The nurse came in with a pair of giant silver scissors, that's when Cinnamon eyes opened wider than a garage. "Where are you going with those big things!?" she asked, as she finally pulled out that rubber band she had been struggling to remove.

The nurse walked up to her after placing on a pair of rubber gloves.

She reached into the middle of Cinnamon hair and grabbed a thick amount of it. "Hold up, lady."

"Don't you think that's too much?" asked Cinnamon. "Miss, I have been doing this for twenty-six years. I can do this blind-folded too. Now, do you mind turning to the left please," said the nurse.

Cinnamon turned around and rolled her eyes, thinking to herself that this lady better talk to her nicely. The nurse cut a big chunk of Cinnamon's hair. It had to be four inches, and it was a thick amount of hair that was removed from Cinnamon's head. Disappointed, she could feel a little bald spot in the center of her head.

"Only for my kids!" she told herself as she put her hair back in a ponytail. She watched the nurse place her hair in a plastic bag and sealed it shut before Cinnamon could think of this important question to ask. "So, how long does it take for the results to come back?" she asked in a low-pitch tone.

"Well, it can take up to three to four weeks, and you will be notified as soon as it's available." "Wow, I thought it would be a lot sooner, but okay. Thanks a lot. I will be looking for your call."

When Cinnamon walked outside, she noticed Levi parked inside of the parking lot. She totally forgot that she asked him to come pick her up. As she walked to his truck, she could hear him listening to *"The Temptation Imagination."*

She opened the truck door and hopped, "Hi boo, I missed you baby. How are you feeling?" "I'm a little hungry, you want something to eat?? Levi asked. "Hell yeah, I'm starving. Let's go to that Chinese buffet," Cinnamon suggested.

As usual Levi agreed with anything Cinnamon asked for. They pulled up to the restaurant, walked in, and were seated at a table.

"This is the perfect place to discuss how we will get rid of mother dearest. I need a gun," Cinnamon said to Levi, not realizing the waitress was standing behind her until the waitress asked if she could get them something to drink. "Yes, two sprites," Levi said to the young blond Chinese waitress. "Let's go get our food, so we can eat and discuss what we need to discuss," said Cinnamon. By the time they filled their plates and sat down their drinks were already on the table.

"Okay, since today is Friday, we will pull up on her on Sunday in the middle of the night. I need for you to have me throw away burner by Sunday, no revolvers. Everyone in that house must die, so I need you to have my back and come inside with me. Make sure you have your burner as well and be ready. No pussy shit, Levi!!!! You said you were a ruthless killer ; you said you love me so I want you to prove it."

They sat there and talked about the entire plan. "See, mother dearest has a weakness and her weakness is gambling. She went to bingo like clockwork every Sunday at the same time."

"Okay, we will catch her on Sunday on bingo day!" She normally comes home between 10:30-11:00 p.m. You and I will be down the block, parked, so we can watch her pull up.

"Just tell me what you need me to do!" Do you want me to sneak up behind her when she puts her keys in the door? Blow her brains out right there?" Levi asked Cinnamon as he pulled his gun out of his pants and gave it a kiss. As he took a sip of his soda, she looked at him like he was nuts to do what he just did in the restaurant.

Thankfully, no one was paying attention. Levi was the kind of man who didn't take any orders from anyone. He was always ready for some action; it seemed like he got a rush out of causing pain to other people.

After eating and discussing their plan for another hour, Levi decided to drop Cinnamon off at her house. They had two days to prepare themselves, and he couldn't wait to go home to clean his guns.

As usual, to relax, Cinnamon took a hot forty-five-minute shower. That's when a thought came to her, and she was surprised she didn't think of it sooner. After mother dearest was officially out of the picture, where would I go? I will be on the run with my boys looking over my shoulder.

Cinnamon was sick and tired of The Claiborne County court system. They made her feel as though they didn't like outsiders; she felt like she was being bullied.

Friday and Saturday came and went so fast that before Cinnamon knew it, Sunday was here and it was time to take things into her own hands and get her kids back with her. The court seemed to be playing games, and Cinnamon wasn't going to sit by it. She was going to get her kids, no matter what she had to do.

It was 9:30 when Levi pulled up to Cinnamon apartment. When she got in his Cadillac, he was playing Tupac's , "*Hit 'em up.*"

She looked at him like he was losing his mind. What was even funnier was that he wore a turtleneck shirt; she hadn't seen one of those in decades. The both of them agreed on wearing all-black ensemble which had Levi looking like a snack over there.

"Here, baby girl," said Levi as he passed Cinnamon a pint of Hennessy which was her favorite drink. "Omg!!! You had to have read my mind," she shouted as she grabbed the bottle out of his hands. She looked in the back seat of the car to grab a cup. As she grabbed the bag of cups, under was a chrome 9mm gun.

The ride there was smooth and quiet as they drove the back road to Claiborne County. By the time they arrived, the Hennessy had Cinnamon feeling nice. Cinnamon looked at the clock on the radio which read 10:17 p.m. A few minutes later, they pulled up to an abandoned brick house which was two blocks down from mother dearest house. "Listen, I've decided that I will be the one to go inside. You wait out here for me," said Cinnamon.

Thirty-five minutes later, they spotted mother's dearest red Chrysler 300 pulled into her driveway.

They watch as she and her daughter enter the house. "Give them enough time to get settled," said Levi, as he rubbed both of his hands together.

A black expedition pulled into the driveway ten minutes after mother dearest pulled up. The front door opened and mother dearest daughter and granddaughter walked out the house and into the black expedition. Cinnamon and Levi watched as the black truck left the house.

Cinnamon looked at the clock and it read 12:30 a.m. Two hours passed by, and she noticed all the lights off in the house. She looked at Levi and said, "I'm ready, so pull up closer to the house, keep the car running." She stepped out of the car and slowly Walked to the back of the house.

The back door was unlocked, as usual, so Cinnamon quietly walked right in. Upon entering through the back door, she was a bit nervous because she was about seven feet away from mother dearest's bedroom. Mother dearest husband worked in a different city every weekend which meant that tonight she was in bed alone. The only people there were her and Cinnamon's two boys.

Levi insisted and practically begged her to put a potato on the tip of the gun as a silencer, so she did just that. He was more experienced at this than her.

Gun in hand, she cocked it back as she got closer to mother dearest's room. "Okay, Cinnamon you could do this," she said to herself as she quietly opened the door.

She tiptoed slowly and quietly as possible. Once she reached the bed, she placed the gun in mother dearest's face. "I'm not to be fucked with," she whispered as she placed both hands on the gun and was ready to squeeze the trigger. Something happened that was unexplainable, this funny feeling that she never felt before came over her mind, body, and soul.

The decision she was about to make was going to change her life and her perception of life forever. She had to make a decision that would not only affect her but her kids as well. Her next move would be an unexpected one.

CHAPTER 14

CRUNCH TIME

Levi sat in his truck wearing a white and lavender three piece custom tailored suit with white alligator shoes. He reached to the right side of him, grabbed his cell phone and dialed Cinnamon's number. "Hello my beautiful queen, I'm on my way to come get you, I will be there in twenty minutes. "Levi it's 10:30a.m, Court doesn't start until 2p.m".

She hated to be rushed, but couldn't complain because Levi was driving her sixty miles there and sixty miles back for free. Twenty minutes flew by like the wind, and before she knew it, Levi was blowing up her phone telling her to come outside.

Cinnamon grabbed her cell phone, placed it in her purse, and walked outside. The weather was so perfect she couldn't help but notice how much of a typical sunny day it was.

Approaching Levi's truck she slowly opened the passenger side door, climbed inside and snapped on her seatbelt.

She glanced over in Levi's direction and couldn't help but notice how he thought he was some cool guy sitting over there bobbing his head, snapping his fingers to the beat of the infamous Sam Cooke , "*Bring it on home*

to me." He was smelling good, looking super fly, and Cinnamon was highly impressed.

Levi put his truck in drive and headed towards the highway. "I see you got good taste in music," Cinnamon jokingly told Levi. He looked at her as if he was about to respond, but said nothing at all. "Why are you staring at me like that?" Cinnamon curiously asked him.

He was deeply in love with Cinnamon, he absolutely adored her. Cinnamon on the other hand wasn't thinking about love at all, she had love for Levi, but clearly not as much love as he had for her.

Her primary focus was regaining custody of her children; anything else besides that had to take a back seat.

The whole ride there, they enjoyed classic hits from the 60's and 70's such as The Temptation, Aretha Franklin, and Marvin Gaye. Cinnamon was infatuated with the 60's, some would say she had an old soul. From the death of Martin Luther King Jr, Malcom X, John. F Kennedy all the way to fashion. Long skirts in earthy colors or with patterns, such as flowers and paisley, along with peasant-type blouses, she knew about it all.

"*Welcome to Port Gibson* " *was* the welcoming sign located on the side of the highway. Underneath that sign read "Too beautiful to burn"

During the war, the city was spared destruction following the Battle of Port Gibson, since, as legend has it, General Ulysses S. Grant said that it was "too beautiful to burn."

Upon arrival Levi pulled up to the court house, placed the car in parked and turned down the music. "Well lady, I will be right here when you come out."

She and Levi locked eyes and smiled at one another before she exited the truck. Cinnamon walked across the street to the Courthouse like she was auditioning for America's Next Top Model.

As she seductively walked into the courtroom, the first face she noticed was Nate's. She couldn't help but to roll her eyes as far back in her head as they would go. past him as if he didn't exist.

"Oh so you can't speak to your husband now? Oh, I see how it is, wifey," Nate, sarcastically said as he watched her pass by him as if he didn't exist. Cinnamon politely walked past him, and headed over to where her law. "Hello Mrs. Cinnamon, how are you today?" Her lawyer asked with a big, bright smile on her face

Her lawyer was a slim, African—American, middle-aged, light-skinned woman who had a heart of gold. "I'm feeling really anxious. all I want is my kids home with me." "Well we did everything that was required, so let's calm down," her lawyer calmly told her.

"You're right. Thanks a lot. Excuse me, while I go sit this behind in a seat," Cinnamon said to her lawyer as she walked in the waiting area. She could see mother dearest and papa sitting in the rear of the courtroom.

Cinnamon decided to sit three rows in front of them. Things couldn't get any uglier because within a couple of minutes, Nate walked in and sat in the same row as Cinnamon exactly four seats down from her.

"Fucking goofy," Cinnamon mumbled as she watched Nate sit there looking like he was the man of the year foh . The sight of his face made her nauseous.

Not long after Nate walked in and took a seat, the judge walked out and everyone stood up. "This court is in session docket number 99877655 in the custody hearing of Cinnamon vs The Department of Human Services. You may be seated,"

While everyone sat down, Cinnamon could see her lawyer waving her hand telling Cinnamon to come sit up front closer to her. Cinnamon didn't hesitate; she did exactly what she was told. Her lawyer looked at her and gave her a smile and a pat on her shoulder.

Cinnamon was puzzled because she could've sworn that The Department of Human Services was no longer involved with her case.

"Judge, we are here today because my client wishes to regain full custody of her children.

A year ago, you granted temporary custody to their grandmother and grandfather. My client has relocated, got a job, and an apartment. She also has six-months worth of random drug screening."

"With that being said, my client wishes to regain full custody of her two children. To Cinnamon's surprise the case workers from DHS were in court as well. Later on, she found out that the judge requested for them to come. "Okay, that's great to hear, but I will need more than these documents to determine if your client is going to regain full custody of her kids. The judge turned to his left to face the caseworkers. "I will need y'all to go view and take pictures of the apartment."

"Court will resume in ninety days," the judge said as he banged his gavel down as hard as he could. Disappointment was written all over Cinnamon's face. She thought for sure that she would be bringing her kids back home with her. Unfortunately, she thought wrong. "It's okay, you're going to get your kids back. Don't worry," said her lawyer as she tried her best to make her feel better but it was useless.

Cinnamon looked over at mother dearest and them. It was crazy how she was dressed. Over there looking like tweety-birds grandma with those oversized glasses, damn near bigger than her face. Cinnamon walked toward the exit and out of the courthouse while noticing mother dearest standing by the elevator with this little smirk on her face.

She walked right past her as if she didn't exist. "I can't stand that bitch," Cinnamon said to herself as she hopped into Levi's truck.

"Are you okay? what's wrong?" he asked. "That damn judge wants to see for himself how the house looks so he asked the social workers from DHS to make a home visit," Cinnamon narrated. We are scheduled to come back to court in ninety days!"

"I know that you are upset but trust me everything will be okay," Levi hated to see Cinnamon upset. He knew how much her kids meant to her. "Let's go grab a bite to eat. I can use a good meal right about now," he told her as he cranked up the car and pulled off.

They pulled up into a Chinese buffet in Jackson Ms. After being seated, Cinnamon watched two little boys around the same age as her boys playing with their toy truck. She couldn't stop the tears from falling from her eyes as she hopelessly watched the boys hanging out with their mother. She got up and ran into the ladies room crying uncontrollably.

She sat on the toilet and cried her eyes out not realizing that some-one walked in the restroom a minute or two behind her. "Excuse me, are you okay?" the nosy old lady asked, feeling a bit concerned. "Yes, I'm fine, thanks," Cinnamon responded, without realizing how loud she was crying. The lady then walked into one of the empty bathroom stalls. Feeling ashamed, and embarrassed, Cinnamon rushed out of the restroom as fast as her body would move, and quickly sat back down at the table.

She and Levi talked about various different topics while enjoying a delicious meal together for about 2 hours before deciding to depart. Afterwards he dropped Cinnamon off at home, gave her a kiss on the forehead and went home.

Three weeks went by and the case worker was scheduled to come make a home visit. The case worker called Cinnamon around 9:00 that morning to inform her that she would be arriving at her residence around 11a.m. This was the same case worker who was cool with mother dearest. Out of the three case workers this lady had to be the one to make the home visit smmfh. Cinnamon made sure to have the boys room overly furnished. Flat screen tv on the wall, bunk beds with comforter sets of the boys favorite cartoon characters, video games, and a closet full of brand new outfits. Her apartment was flawless; she was overly prepared for this day. An hour flew by when Cinnamon heard someone knocking at the door. "Coming!!!" she yelled excitedly running to the door.

"Hello Cinnamon, I'm here on a court order to view the apartment," the case worker said as if Cinnamon didn't already know this. "Well, come on in and let me give you a grand tour", Cinnamon told her. "This is the boys room, my oldest will get the bottom bunk and my youngest will be on top," she said as she pointed to the bunk beds.

Nice, I love the sponge bob sheets," she stated prior to pulling out her cell phone to snap pictures."This is the bathroom, and my room is right here, and the kitchen is on the left." The case worker snapped pictures of every angle of the house. Before leaving, she gave Cinnamon a fake speech on how proud she was of her accomplishments.

Cinnamon wasn't trying to hear it though she knew it was bullshit. This was coming from the same caseworker who told Cinnamon she had to continue her marriage to Nate in order to get her kids back.

Time was flying by extremely fast, and before Cinnamon knew it, it was time to go back to court. Cinnamon knew for a fact that this was it; this time around her kids will be in her custody. The judge required her to take a random drug test every week, get a job, and a place to live.

Cinnamon had all three; she was also in school for the position and study of a Dental Assistant. Levi made plans for the boys to go to a water park the following weekend. He wanted to do something nice to welcome them back home.

"Well, this is it, baby girl. I'll be right here when you come out." Cinnamon stepped out of the truck and walked across the street to the courthouse. She was super excited and proud of herself. She couldn't wait to see the expression on mother 's dearest face when the judge award custody back to Cinnamon.

When she walked into the court room she saw the two caseworkers, district attorney, and mother dearest, all huddled together, having a conversation. Her lawyer waved at her to come and sit next to her so she started to walk in that direction. "What the hell are they talking about?" she asked as she sat down next to her lawyer.

I don't know that's not my concern. My concern is you." Cinnamon looked at her and smiled. She then realized that her lawyer was a cool, calm, and collective woman, and at that moment, she realized that she really liked this lady.

"All rise. Docket number 67906543 in a custody hearing for Cinnamon vs The Department of Human Services," the security said. The judge walked out and after sitting down, he told everyone to take a seat.

The judges looked at the caseworkers and asked "Okay, first I would like to know if you visited Cinnamon's apartment and what evidence you have to back it up?" "Yes, your honor. I have taken a trip to her apartment and photos of the entire apartment have been taken. We have those pictures here if you would like to see them," said one of the caseworkers.

"Can you grab those for me?" said the judge as he looked to the left of him at the bailiff who was standing there like a statue. "No problem, sir," said the bailiff as he walked over to the table where the case worker was sitting, grabbed the paperwork, and then handed it to the judge.

As the judge opened the folder, Cinnamon turned around to take a glance at the expression on mother's dearest face.

As she turned around, it seemed like mother dearest was thinking the same thing because she locked eyes with her instantly.

The judge had an aura as if he was surprised by Cinnamon's accomplishments. When she left Port Gibson to get herself together, no one thought she would come back with a bang. They were wrong, and they underestimated her strength, that's for damn sure.

"Okay, so I'm looking over everything, and there is something here that doesn't add up," the judge said. *Here we go with the fuckery,* Cinnamon thought to herself. She wanted to jump up and be ratchet, but decided not to besides that would only make things worse.

Your lease shows that the total amount of rent is $595 a month. Then there's a light bill every month, water billphone bill, and household supplies. Your total income per month by the looks of your check stubs isn't enough to pay for your finances let alone two children.

Judge, may I address the court?" requested Cinnamon's lawyer. When he shook his head up and down she began to speak. "Judge, I understand what you're saying, but we have to considered the fact my client is working two part time jobs while attending college."

"Yes, but you don't understand that having two children is a big responsibility. I have to be sure that if her kids return to her they will have stability."

He looked over at the caseworker and asked if they had anything to add. "As a matter of fact, we do your honor. The Department of Human Services would like to request a hair sample drug screening. We want to make sure that Cinnamon is 100 percent sober and free of any narcotics."

Cinnamon could hear mother dearest back there running her big ass mouth in agreement, but decided not to say anything.

"I agree, so with that being said, we will return in ninety days. I'm requesting your client to bring the hair sample as well proof that she will be able to financially support her children," the judge said. Well judge, my client isn't the only parent involved, they also have a father who is required to financially provide for them as well. Not only that, but your honor, should he not be required to submit to a drug screening as well?" her lawyer questioned.

"Nate, do you have anything to say?" "Yes, judge to be honest, I'm not in any position to even think about regaining custody," said Nate.

"Does that answer your question?" the judge asked as he grabbed his gavel while looking at Cinnamon's lawyer. He banged it down like he was trying to break a rock into a million pieces. "This case will continue in ninety days."

Cinnamon couldn't decide if she wanted to smack her lawyer, the judge, that caseworker or smack the hell out of mother dearest no two front teeth having ass.

"This some fucking bullshit!" Cinnamon angrily yelled as she jumped out of her seat and stormed out of the courtroom.

Nate got up and followed her to the elevator to try to see where her head was at. He slowly crept up behind her, and whispered in her ear, "I *miss you, wifey*,". "Get the hell away from me. I'm not falling for your manipulations, Nate."

She couldn't stand the thought of being too close to him. "Oh, and by the way, your mother is going to wish she never crossed me. Mark my words," Cinnamon said as she angrily walked onto the elevator,and exited the CourtHouse.

Levi could tell by Cinnamon's demeanor that it didn't go well.

"I want her dead. I want her fucking dead," said Cinnamon as she got into Levi's truck. "What happened? Baby calm down and talk to me," Levi told her. Cinnamon took a deep breath before looking Levi in his eyes and said ask"You said you love me and you would do anything for me right?" "RIGHT?!!

Levi looked at her and said " I will do anything, for you my love, just tell me and your wish will be my command."

"I want that old bitch DEAD!!!!" Cinnamon shouted as loud as she could.

Cinnamon was tired of being played for weak, it was time mother dearest got what she deserves. It was time she met her motherfucking maker. She messed with the wrong one, and it was time she paid for it.

"Levi pulled out his 38 snub nose revolver and opened the driver side of the door of his truck. He was ready to shut this little town the fuck down. He was a beast, you know the type of beast who was so good at what he did that he never got caught.

Within a matter of seconds he transformed into a monster, better yet a killer. The look in his eyes was pure evil and demonic . "I'm on it; today I will prove my love to you." Just stay right here and keep the truck running. Don't leave this truck, understand?" Levi asked.

"Yes, I understand," Cinnamon told him. Levi walk towards the courthouse.

Suddenly out of nowhere Cinnamon's stomach began to turn flips, at the same time she was feeling nauseating.

Something horrible was about to happen and she had to ask herself if she was sure about what she was asking Levi to do for her. Was she mentally prepared to subdue the consequences of her actions?

CHAPTER 15

BREAKING THE CURSE

Faith without work is dead and if you want something in this world you have to fight for it. You have to get up off your ass and go get it. If you think that someone is going to hand it to you on a silver platter, then you're living in a fucking fairytale. Your best hope is to keep fighting until you cannot fight anymore. Even at this state of exhaustion from battling your demons you still have to find the strength to get up and keep going.

Cinnamon couldn't see herself putting her kids through the same pain, suffering and abuse she went through. A murder case would definitely be the cause of that.

Killing mother dearest would only bring forth negative energy. She was no killer; she was just a woman who would kill for what belonged to her if necessary.

The ride back home was awkwardly silent, and Levi was extremely quiet which was abnormal. it was obvious that he had a lot on his mind. What Cinnamon didn't know is that Levi loved her so much that he would do anything to make sure she was happy, even kill!!

When she arrived home, she laid flat on her back gazing up at the ceiling, until she fell asleep.

The next morning Cinnamon received some news that left her stunned.

Her lawyer informed her that the caseworker who visited her apartment was subsequently fired. "Are you serious?" Cinnamon stated.

She was so surprised that she couldn't help but to let out a laugh as an expression of happiness.

"God don't like ugly; that lady got what she deserved

She fed Cinnamon false information when she told her that she had to stay with Nate in order to get custody of her children.. "It was like she hated women because they were able to do what she was unable to do … give birth to a child."

With the caseworker out of the picture, Cinnamon had a higher chance of gaining full custody of her boys.

The next day, Levi picked Cinnamon up from work and took her out to dinner. In the middle of eating dinner, Cinnamon's mind begins to wander. She daydreamed about her life and the history of African—Americans as a whole. Over 100 years ago, women didn't have any rights; they were programmed to speak, talk and dress a certain way.

Women across the world risked their lives and freedom so women today could have a voice. Cinnamon had one question for herself "If you were in front of Harriet Tubman, would you be proud of the way you're living your life or would you be ashamed?" Her answer was self-explanatory; she followed the same footsteps as her mother, the person she vowed to never become. Losing custody of her kids due to substance abuse along with staying in an abusive relationship spoke for itself. Oblivious to the fact that her actions along with her destructiveness caused the cycle to repeat itself. Most people would have called it a family curse or better yet, ancestral sin, or generational curse. It is the doctrine that individuals inherit the judgment for the sin of their ancestors. It exists primarily as a concept in Mediterranean religions; generational sin is referenced in the Bible in Exodus 20:5.

Cinnamon had to get her life on track and pursue happiness not only for herself and her kids but for her ancestors who paved the way for her to be phenomenal. Tears ran down her face as she continued to reminisce on her life and the choices she's made over the last few years. There's no one to blame about the outcome of her life but herself. She realized when she stopped praying, going to church, reading the Bible and living right, she got negative results out of life. When she lived in sin, life was hell. In other words if you live your life in darkness, you attract negativity. If it so happens that you navigate through life in the light of purity, positive things will gravitate towards you. The awesomeness of this theology is that we have the freedom of choice.

"What's up, girl?" What are you over there day-dreaming about ?" Levi jokingly asked when he notice Cinnamon was more quiet than usual.

"Nothing Levi, I'm just thinking about my life and why I'm going through so much difficulties." He looked her in the eyes and said, "Our mistakes in life are what makes us stronger and wiser. Embrace life's challenges and look at it as an opportunity to be a warrior."

"I don't know what I will do without you Levi, you've been here for me when I didn't have anyone and for that I appreciate you from the bottom of my heart." Cinnamon meant every word, and without Levi her custody battle would have been disastrous. She stood up out of her seat to give Levi a kiss on the forehead. "Now, let's get out of here," Cinnamon said as she grabbed her sweater off the back of her chair.

The drive home was smooth and relaxing. They listened to Jackie Wilson and enjoyed each other's vibe.

The first time she listened to Jackie Wilson's *"Lonely Teardrops"* was when she was eleven years old living in Mississippi with Mona. One Saturday afternoon Jackie Wilson music video popped up on the television advertising his album. The melody hit her soul, took away her anxiety, and helped wash away the pain, hurt, and loneliness. Funny how times fly when you keep yourself occupied.

Court came around so quickly Cinnamon was amazed at how fast time flew by. Her knees were sore from all the praying she was doing. She decided to let go and let God take over.

Levi was on his way to pick her up and take her to court. When he arrived, all he could talk about was other options to getting her kids back permanently. "I think you should let me send mother dearest to her maker," said Levi as he made a shooting sound while holding his hand, pretending it was a gun. Levi looked at her and said, "POW." He couldn't help himself he miss putting in work and causing hell.

They pulled up in front of the courthouse, and as soon as Cinnamon got out of the car, all eyes were on her.

She made sure she looked extra gorgeous dressed like a celebrity from head to toe. Her hair was laced with an Brazilian lace front, her lashes, and make up were on fleek. She wore her best outfit: a pow-der-pink blazer pants suit with powder-pink stilettos.

Cinnamon walked inside the courtroom, and the first face she noticed was Nate sitting there beside his mother.

"Hi, beautiful," said Cinnamon as she walked up to her lawyer. "Hello girl, and I must say that you look amazing," her lawyer told her.

"Next case is number 197543334 custody hearing. Your honor-able judge is in session,"As the judge walked in the courtroom, the hair on Cinnamon's neck began to stand up.

Afterwards, came this cool feeling of ease and warmth. Cinnamon's lawyer looked up at the judge and began to speak. "Your honor, I have here with me as requested by the courts." She gathered all the paper-work together before handing it to the judge. "My client had taken the hair samples required, she also has checked stubs from her first and second job. My client has done everything asked of her, your honor."

The judge quietly looked through paperwork that was handed to him, then he looked up at the case worker before asking his question. "Does the Department of Human Service have anything to add?"

The caseworkers looked at each other before telling the judge that they had nothing to add. The judge then looked in mother dearest and Nate's direction before asking if there was anything that they wanted to add.

Cinnamon took a deep breath because she knew that the devil had a hold on mother dearest, he could get her to do whatever he asked of her.

Cinnamon noticed Nate holding his head down shaking it left and right implying that he had nothing to say. He knew for a fact that his mother was about to say something to make Cinnamon look like the worst parent ever.

"Yes, your honor, I want to add something," she said while looking at Cinnamon. I'm sick of all this back and forth and in and out of court. I would like to turn over my grandchildren to their mother. I just want to be a grandma." Everyone's mouth fell to the floor, no one expected her to say what she said.

Mother dearest has done everything in her power to keep this woman away from her children for no serious reason at all. She hated Cinnamon with a passion and would probably spit on Cinnamons grave if she was to die.

The judge looked at mother dearest as if she was speaking a foreign language. "Can you repeat what you said, ma'am?" the judge curiously asked. Mother dearest looked at the judge and slowly stated, "I would rather be a grandma to my grandkids. I want those handsome boys with their mama."

All of the things that Cinnamon experienced such as her being taken away from her mother at two, her being sexually and physically abused, her attempt suicide at eleven, along with trauma after trauma, made her stronger than ever. There was nothing that she couldn't fight for,better yet nothing that she couldn't withstand. Her pain reversed itself into strength, it built her faith, it made her what she was striving to be, which was a strong, black woman!

"It's granted. Full custody to the mother!!!!" the judge stated before banging down his gavel. Cinnamon couldn't believe her ears. Her prayers had finally been answered, and finally she would be reunited with her kids.Cinnamon began to cry tears of joy as she stood up and squeezed the hell out of her Lawyer. For if it wasn't for Cinnamon's faith and patience she would have lost her mind a long time ago.

Court was over, and Cinnamon couldn't wait to share the news with Levi. When she made it outside to his car the side door was unlocked, but Levi was nowhere in sight.

Fifteen minutes went by, and still no Levi, getting a little impatient,Cinnamon decided to turn on the car radio.

The infamous Mary J Blidge's, *"Not gon cry"* was playing. As soon as she started to bob her head to the music, she noticed mother dearest and her husband exiting the CourtHouse walking to their vehicle.

Next thing you know, out of nowhere, Levi hopped into the car breathing heavily, smelling like gasoline. "Hi, baby girl. Don't worry, everything is taken care of. I told you I'm here for you. All your worries will soon be gone," Levi anxiously stated while staring in the direction of Mother Dearest's car.

He was sitting in the driver seat with this smirk on his face. Within the next five seconds there was a big "KABOOM".

Mother dearest car blew up, her shit exploded into pieces. Cinnamon's heart began to beat rapidly, and her ears were ringing from the explosion. Levi didn't say a word instead he crunked up, and quickly sped off.

"Did this mother fucker do what I think he did?"

is the question that Cinnamon asked herself. She desperately wanted to ask Levi,but was afraid to ask. Levi didn't say anything about the incident, it was as if he was in another dimension. To be honest Cinnamon already knew the answer to that question and decided to not mention it. Besides, she just won the war against mother dearest. That moment meant everything to her. Who cares if he tried to intimidate mother dearest by blowing up her car. Hell, she'd been intimidating Cinnamon for years.She was definitely wrong to think that Cinnamon wasn't going to put up a fight for her two boys. She truly felt that Cinnamon was weak and incompetent. The drive back was a little awkward and silent with no mention about what had occurred.

The next week, mother dearest was on her way to permanently drop the boys off. The drop off location was at the police station in Rankin County at the judge's request. All of the hard work that Cinnamon put into regaining custody of her children has paid off. After loading the boys up in the car she hugged and kissed the both of them for what seemed like eternity.

She instantly had a heavy load lifted from off her shoulders. The storm was over and she felt happier than ever.

Leaving Mississippi and all the drama that came with it was her number one priority.

Levi wasn't jovial about her decision to relocate, instead he insisted on her and the boys moving in with him, but Cinnamon politely declined.She was ready to turn over a new leaf, and start her life all over again.

Moving back to New York where there were better opportunities for her boys who were now 6 and 9 years old was at the top of her list. That was her main focus and priority at that moment.

Driving off into the beautiful sunset, Levi looked over at Cinnamon and told her how proud he was and how much he loved her.

THE END

ABOUT THE AUTHOR

Cynthia A. Thomas, born and raised in the Bronx, New York, is the author of *Cinnamon*, a book that illuminates her journey through mental health struggles. As a certified professional in Dental, Administrative, and Nursing fields, she used her experiences to break free from her own limitations. Her passion for creative writing, discovered in her youth, became her refuge during her battle with depression. Her book, *Poetic Agony*, serves as a blueprint for resilience, inspiring others to overcome their challenges. Cynthia's message is one of hope, encouraging her readers to embrace life, love, and happiness, regardless of their struggles.

Milton Keynes UK
Ingram Content Group UK Ltd.
UKHW030909141024
449705UK00013B/647